Flight From Munich

Hello Hubert + Hazel
Best wishes from
Don Toye

**FAIRWINDS/CDA
LIBRARY**

Flight From Munich

Donald Toye

*Formerly
Lt. Toye, U.S. Eighth Air Force
445th Bombardment Group
703rd Squadron
United Kingdom*

**Northwest Publishing Inc.
Salt Lake City, Utah**

Flight from Munich

All rights reserved.
Copyright © 1993 NPI

Reproductions in any manner, in whole or in part,
in English or in other languages, or otherwise
without written permission of the publisher is prohibited.

For information address: Northwest Publishing,
5949 South 350 West, Salt Lake City, Utah 84107

SM/LC 10 1 93

PRINTING HISTORY
First Printing 1994

ISBN: 1-56901-082-X

NPI books are published by Northwest Publishing Incorporated,
5949 South 350 West, Salt Lake City, Utah 84107.
The name "NPI" and the "NPI" logo are trademarks belonging to
Northwest Publishing Incorporated.

PRINTED IN THE UNITED STATES OF AMERICA.
10 9 8 7 6 5 4 3 2 1

Illustrations

Lt. Donald Toye ix
Bomber Path and Escape Route xi
Clarence M. Wieseckel..11
B-24 Bomber Crew 12
B-24 Liberator 18
The Fairons...62
House like Fairon house in Luxembourg 106
Joe Kerpan and Bob Korth 130
Leo Carey's Gravestone 194

Foreword

In World War II, Lieutenant Donald Toye and Sergeant Clarence Wieseckel, fliers from separate downed bombers, met in a Partisan camp in the Belgian Black Forest. With the help of farmers and the "Underground," they walked across France to reach safety in Switzerland. While there, Toye began writing an account of their experiences but was returned to service by General Patton's men before he completed it. Interrupted again after the war ended, by home and family in Portland, Oregon claiming his attention, he let the manuscript gather dust in closets over the years. It wasn't until he learned of Clarence Wieseckel's death thirty-seven years later that he felt compelled to pick up the work from where he left off and complete it for the benefit of the Wieseckel, and his own, family's enjoyment.

Thinking in retrospect about his and Clarence's successful journey, Toye developed the strong notion that an innate spiritually motivated goodness in Clarence might somehow have been responsible for giving them Divine guidance. It seemed to him that adventures they had together, so scary that they had a fictional flavor, nearly always turned out to have happy endings. Although these things were mystical to him, it seemed that Clarence took them for granted, as if he knew all along what the turnout would be. In hindsight to Toye, it appeared their paths had crossed for some benevolent reason, and that Clarence had arrived "from out of nowhere," coming to assure the success of a perilous journey through enemy lines. Out of deference to him then, Toye wanted to title his book *Johnny,* a name bestowed on Clarence by the Belgian Army Blanche. As the story unfolded, however, no clear portrait of *Johnny* seemed to delineate—thus, the title *Flight from Munich*, which seemed apropos of Toye's experience.

"Co-Pilot - Ship #132
Nine Yanks and a Jerk"

Lt. Donald Toye
703rd Squadron, 445th Bomb Group
Tibenham, United Kingdom

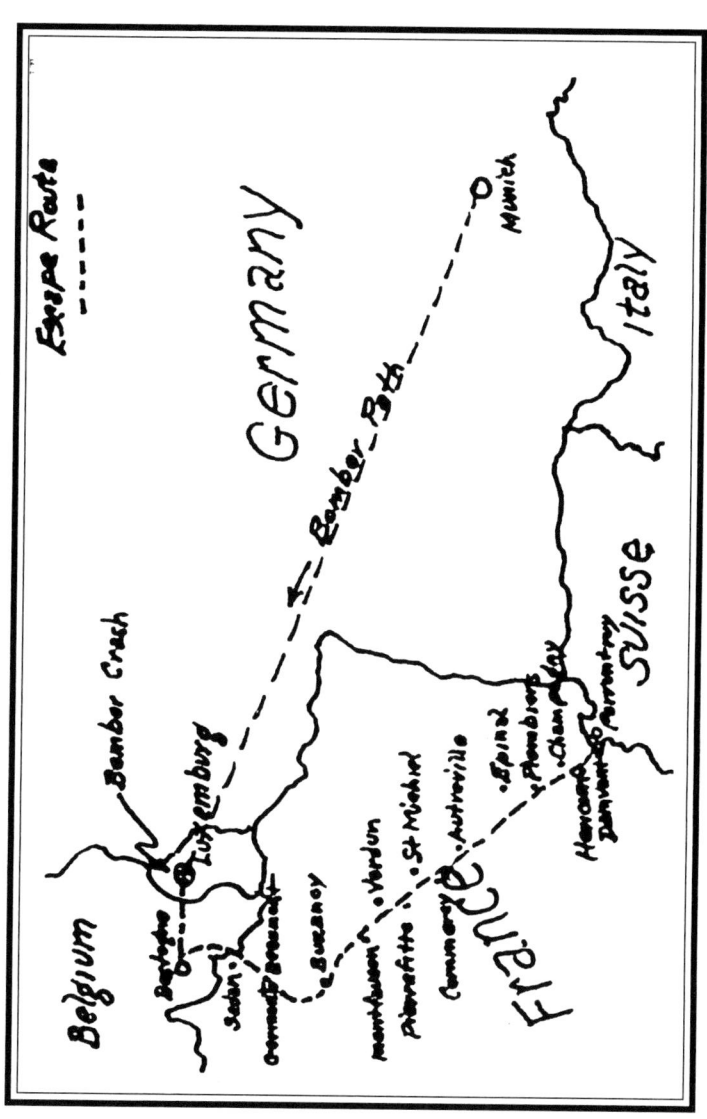

Map of Bomber Path and Escape Route

Prisoners of the Swiss

Late in June of 1944 our Allies, advancing from out of their Normandy beachheads, had softened Nazis European defenses and would soon bring World War II to an end. From the beaches' south end and hardly noticed at first, General Patton's Seventh Army took off in a swift encircling sweep through southern France all the way to Lyon, little more than a stone's throw from the border of Switzerland. Radio broadcasts from London cleverly played down this bold stroke and continued to talk only about the savage fighting around Normandy. But, in the little Swiss town of Glion, where we "Escapees" waited for news that would take us back to our outfits in England, grapevine gossip had it that the Allies were already knocking at the gates of Paris. Prospects of history ever recording a victory as fantastic as this happening so soon after D-Day were pretty slim indeed, but that made little difference to our wild bunch of detainees at de Glion Hotel. Hell bent to get back to someplace we could call home, we wanted to believe that our troops had reached Paris—whether it was true or not. To us this luscious tidbit of news meant that we'd be getting back sooner. We had escaped from our downed aircraft behind German lines, made our way across occupied territory and now, in our Swiss haven of escape, were fighting desperate boredom. An abrupt halt to such high-spirited action in aerial combat put us into a mood of restlessness, as we waited to return home. For some of our group the months had stretched into years.

Glion, a Swiss village in the Alps, is high above Lake Geneva and looks directly down on Byron's famed Chillon Prison. In peacetime, wealthy English and American retirees, in search of prestigious enjoyment, had discovered this picturesque Shangri-La, but when war began, Switzerland was surrounded by the Axis enemy and Glion's posh hotels emptied. The Allied governments, in search of a place to bivouac their growing number of displaced fliers, found them a convenient source of housing for the four hundred or so "Escapees." These were British or American fliers who had crash landed or parachuted into enemy territory, then escaped across a neutral border to safety. As residents of the hotels where our American groups were billeted, we were free to return to our bases just as soon as Allied forces cleared a pathway to the Swiss border.

"Internees," on the other hand, were those who had flown their planes directly into neutral countries for asylum. By Geneva Rules they were placed in military encampments, and were to be held there until six months after the end of hostilities. With camps located a good distance from ours at Glion, quite a few hundred of these Internees, dressed in the military uniforms of their respective British or American flying corps, were assigned to military barracks, where they were held under the Swiss military command. Their status under confinement approximated that of prisoners of war—not at all like civilian treatment that we received as Escapees.

As Escapees in Glion who had never had it so good, we nevertheless doubted that the Swiss would return us to active duty, even when their borders were freed. They were died-in-the-wool neutral and, because of their unyielding compliance with the Geneva Rules, we suspected that strong ties with Germany kept them from bending our way. As a result, we were as much prisoners of Glion as Byron's Bonivar was the "prisoner of Chillon."

Lt. Brown, a B-24 Liberator pilot and one of the Escapees, had been transferred to the American Legation in Bern, where he was to have a desk job. We envied him the opportunity to escape the all-consuming boredom. He returned for a visit and we clustered around him hoping to hear all the latest dope. Brown, an amiable good-looking fellow, announced the word was that we wouldn't have to wear American uniforms while at our hotels. "The idea is," he said, "we'll have to wear them the day we leave here."

"What do they think we are, a bunch of goddam internees?" That was Sergeant Joe Coss. He loved to cuss, whether it did any good or not. He also took a great deal of pleasure in denouncing the Swiss inflexibility concerning the Geneva Rules, as did we all. Coss was in the first American crew to arrive in Switzerland over a year before. Counsel General Wood had told him he was actually ashamed that no one but British had come prior to his arrival, for it looked as if the British were fighting the war alone.

"Well, you know how the Swiss are, Joe," said easy-going Brown.

"Yeah, but what the hell," put in Coss.

"Yeah, but what the hell," mimicked Brown with a grin.

Lt. Jack Holton, who had been taking it all in, entered his usual cynical comment. "Christ, you haven't any kick coming, Coss. The officers have to wear G.I. uniforms. They're the ones who've got a right to bitch."

Jack was our only P-38 pilot who successfully made it to Switzerland. Some inept ground chief had sent him out with cardboard shutters covering his engine radiators. One engine overheated and conked out on him. He had to bail out and hoof it. Jack was a highly intelligent fellow and somewhat of a cynic, but usually good natured. He could beat the hell out of me in a game of bridge, but we usually played partners against a couple of R.A.F. friends at des Alps Hotel.

The discussion continued. We knew the Swiss would do just about as they pleased with us. Our Legation never interfered. Diplomatic policy, I guessed. It was boring and only served to intensify the overall frustration. I drifted away from the group.

For over a month I had been looking for a wrist watch for my wife, Jeanne, and had finally found one that I liked at Bornands in Montreux. I was receiving my regular paycheck from the Legation, so I'd have money to pay for it. I decided I'd take a run down and look at it one more time. The funicular dropped me the thousand feet down the mountain to Territet. From there I walked the half kilometer to Montreux. As I passed the Weimgurber, I spied Lieutenants Tony Kosinski, Joe Pavelka and Jim Goebels, sitting at a sidewalk table sheltered by an awning. They were just finishing "Coupe d'Denmarks," the European version, but a poor imitation, of an American chocolate sundae.

The only available chair was opposite Tony and facing the building, leaving me no opportunity to watch the pretty girls go by. There were pretty girls in Switzerland, some a little buxom for my taste, but a welcome relief from the all-male contingent at the hotel.

"Whadda yous tink you're doin'?" asked Tony, using his best Chicago gangster dialect. He was a P-47 pilot I met in Bade Lostorf a month earlier, when we were in quarantine. At the time I hadn't liked him, because he seemed too aloof, as if flying a fighter put him a step above the bomber boys. Since then, his quiet ways of not shooting off his mouth, unless he had something worthwhile to say, had earned my respect. I told him where I was headed, as the waitress came to the table.

"Give me one of these," I said, pointing to the Coupe d'Denmarks.

"One of these," she pronounced carefully. She, like many people in Montreux, could speak English fairly well. The boys all liked her, because she was one of the nice girls in town. There were quite a few who couldn't wear that label.

"Did you buy a watch?" asked Goebels. Swiss watches were on all of our minds. Goebels was a tall slim kid of about twenty and seemed to think that the deep voice he affected gave him added maturity. Like myself, he flew a Lib and loved to talk about airplanes!

"Yeah, I picked out an Omega. I'm really sold on it."

"H-h-how much did you pay for it?" stuttered Joe Pavelka. He was piloting a Lib on his twenty-fourth mission when he went down. One more and he'd have been "home free." A friendly, likeable guy, his focus was on a girl back home.

"Three hundred and forty francs with a five percent discount for cash," I told him.

"I-I- thought you were going to buy that Tivannes." He had bought one for his girl and I had nearly followed suit.

"Yeah, I was pretty sold on that one for awhile but I looked at so many others in a month's time that I got tired of it." I had finished my Coupe d'Denmark, so I paid my bill and left for Bornand's. On the way I ran into Lt. Phil Soloman, Joe's navigator. These two men respected each other to such a degree that one couldn't help admiring them. Phil had a master's degree in accounting along with a great deal of native intelligence, so it was little wonder Joe held him in such high regard. I sometimes felt he was too precise, for I like to speak in generalities.

"Where are you headed?" he asked. He always formed each work consciously, as if he was studying in an elocution class. He was fond of telling the story of how he had parachuted from his plane over France and had the unusual distinction of landing astride a cow. If anyone else had told it, it would have been hilarious but, because of his precise speech and matter-of-fact expression, the humor was lost.

"I'm on my way to pick up a watch I bought. Want to come along?"

"Yes. I'm trying to make up my mind on one too. Maybe yours will give me an idea."

We went on to Bornand's where Phil soon became sold on my watch and ordered one of the same. I felt pretty good about it, because his reputation for caution and precise thoughtfulness somehow gave added credence to the wisdom of my selection.

That evening at dinner in the hotel, Lt. Tucker, a B-24 bombardier, was giving me his usual resume of war news. He had a radio in his room and, when he wasn't running up and down the dials in search of hot band music, he managed to find time to listen to "This is London Calling."

The Americans are cutting off twenty divisions of German troops! Do you realize that that could be three hundred thousand men? Boy! I'm going to start packing. We'll be out of here soon." He could get about as excited over war news as he could over Glenn Miller. Sometimes at the noon meal he would say, "Glenn Miller's on at one o'clock. I've gotta get Kitty on the ball to get the food on the table. I've gotta hear Glenn Miller. I just gotta." He could speak more correctly, but his excitement over the music carried him away.

His almost too perfect features made him less than the ideal of masculine handsomeness. His impulsiveness governed his purse and, as a result, he was always broke and often putting the bite on one of the rest of us for a loan.

Kitty, a Cockney English remnant of better days in this resort village, was a combination receptionist, waitress, barmaid, and general hotel manager. Tips flowed freely from the rich in those days and she no doubt missed them, now that she was nurse-maiding a bunch of soldiers. She was a willowy middle-aged school marm type, to whom all of us became so attached that we thought of her as a housemother. Her raucous voice could be heard from anywhere in the entire hotel and was as much a part of the place as the furnishings themselves.

"Haw, haw, haw," sounded Goebel's forced guffaw at some joke he and Holton shared at their table.

"Boy, I bet he expects an Oscar for that Barrymore performance," Lt. Tucker said in a low sarcastic voice meant only for my ears. He and Goebels had been on the same crew and took pleasure in privately gibing one another.

Captain Johnny Hickman, hotel C.O. because he outranked the rest of us, cast a knowing look in my direction. He sat with Tony Kosinski at the head table near the window which looked out over Lake Geneva.

After dinner, Johnny asked me if I had anything on for the evening, and when I answered in the negative, he invited me to his room for a glass of wine. I kept the date promptly, for I knew we were in for a good bull session.

"By God, this place is the nuts," Johnny laughed. "It's a nightmare in a man's life." He was always good at putting things into their simplest form. We sat for several hours discussing this and that and telling anecdotes of our past life in America.

"You know, Toye, this crazy interlude in Switzerland would make a marvelous story. I'd like to write a book about it," Johnny went on.

"That's my idea, too, Johnny, and I think I'll try my hand at it," I said.

Hickman was referring to just such things as the wild party going on in the hotel. I could hear Sergeant Tony Ornateck's loud voice yelling, "de Glion is a son-of-a-bitch of a place." He was a little tight.

Hickman, a good-looking blonde guy, appreciated a good party too and, on more than one occasion, had been the life of them. He was a Mustang pilot and had that wild uninhibited way of living that motion pictures always give to the heroes of their airplane melodramas. Johnny dispatched his duties at the hotel as they arose, but he far preferred not to be bothered by responsibilities that would tie him down.

I took a run downstairs to the bar room for our next bottle of wine and, while I was there, got an eyeful of the party goers. Tony Ornateck had his eyes half closed and was expounding on the unflattering points of the Swiss. Cotton, so nicknamed for his white hair, was being a good listener, although he looked a little bored in his sobriety. Doyle, usually to be seen with his friend Tony, was contributing his bit to the conversation, but he had to often give way to Tony, who was determined to do most of the talking. Heath, also a little wobbly from drinking, was shooting a game of Alpina billiards with Bob Goddard. Heath was sort of an overbearing garrulous chap, while Bob, the exact opposite, was always good natured or silent. All but Doyle in the billiard room were sergeants.

Another sergeant, whose absence was to be expected, but who provides most to this story, was Clarence Wieseckel. It was not in his nature to be seen in such a disorderly crowd as the one sounding off in the billiard room tonight. He was a quiet man. Clarence, or "Johnny," as I had been calling him, was my partner in our escape across occupied France. Had it not been for the customary protocol that separated officers from enlisted men in the Air Corps, I would have been palling around with him. He was my best friend. It was he, who by his fervent dedication to living the Ten Commandments, more than by any action of mine, brought us through unscathed. I firmly believe this, because I hadn't lived by the Book.

When my bottle of wine came, I went back to Hickman's room. Kosinski and Holton had dropped in to chat away the last minutes of the evening and, when I entered, Johnny was teasing Tony about his actions at Mrs. Lemke's tea that afternoon. Mrs. Lemke was a wealthy American lady who had been stranded in Switzerland since the war started and she had generously contributed to our entertainment by giving a tea for a few officers each Thursday afternoon. Mrs. Lemke's daughter, Molly, had married an Italian and the two of them were always at the teas.

"I didn't mind your telling Mrs. Lemke about how your dog used to stool on the floor, but I did object to your making those cracks about the food," Johnny was saying jokingly to Tony.

"Aw, I didn' do anyting wrong. I just asked her when the main course was comin' on when she gave us them little biscuits," Tony laughed. He was getting a kick out of poking fun at himself, and I believe he actually enjoyed being teased about his Chicago accent.

When the party broke up, I went to my room and found Don just getting in. Lt. Don Smith was my roommate, and we'd had many a friendly argument. Smith had also co-piloted a Lib which crashed and, because he could speak French, had found it a breeze getting from France into Switzerland.

Don was a good roommate for me; we were enough different in our ways to leave each other plenty of privacy. In spite of his many good qualities, he was an admittedly lazy person and continually left his belongings for someone else to pick up. He was the type who never closed a door behind him nor got up enough energy to replenish his stock of cigarettes or razor blades when he ran out. He also had a nervousness which showed up mostly in the way he repeatedly flicked his cigarette with his index finger.

Don exchanged a few more beefs with me about our abhorrence of the excessive prices the hotel charged us for liquor, and we went to bed.

There were others at de Glion worth mentioning, but they were the ones with whom I had only casual acquaintance. The monotony for me was broken by mixing company—a little tennis with Smith, Holton, and Goebels, an occasional bridge game with Holton and two R.A.F. pilot friends bivouacked at des Alps Hotel, sharing a bottle of wine with Hickman or, more enjoyably, relaxing in animated conversation with Soloman and Pavelka.

In our low-keyed existence in such richly-appointed surroundings, there were but two moments of excitement that rudely awakened us to the drama of our recent past. One was an incident when a dogfight between a Messerschmitt and one of our own fighter planes accidentally strayed over our neutral haven at Montreux. While our plane appeared to be getting the worst of it, some of the watching townspeople cheered and clapped; but when a second American pursuit plane dove from above to shoot the Messerschmitt down in flames, the crowd booed. These were the Swiss feelings toward Americans in the German sector. The other incident came when the Nazis burned the homes at St. Gingolph in Italy across the lake from us in order to stamp out resistance by the underground Maquis. The Swiss were in sympathy with that too. The attitude of the Swiss toward the Allies was enough to make us want a breakthrough that would effect our release at the earliest possible moment.

Everyone at de Glion Hotel had a story to tell. Since each of us had shared somewhat equally in excitement, however, we found that the stories of these experiences soon became more or less commonplace. To anyone who had not lived them, however, the stories told by the men at Glion would prove exciting to say the least.

I like to think back on the dramatic events that colored my own life beginning with the raid on Munich, April 13, 1944. It seems to me now that some of the incidents happened ever so long ago, so long in fact that they are more like dreams that one has when he is sick with a fever. And yet, the people who always turned up to rescue me from danger, deprivation, exhaustion, and even illness will always remain as real in my memory as those who lived with me at Glion. Even more explicably, however, is the strange manner in which these people made their timely appearances, when they were most needed. It convinces me that these were not just happenstances and that there must certainly be a God who watches over us. This is such a strong part of my belief that I must chronicle those events, as I remember them. They are as much a part of the war as were the beaches of Normandy, the Battle of the Bulge, and the eventual surrender of the Axis Forces.

Clarence M. Wieseckel

My partner walking across France to Switzerland.
Refused to steal a bicycle.

B-24 Bomber Crew
Second Row - Butler • Lennon • Breckham (shotdown-ME-109) • Kerpan • Standridge • Subar
First Row - Farmer • Toye • Korth • Carey (killed)

Gathering Clouds

Back in England, with the 445th Bombardment Group near Tibenham, Jack Farmer and I began to view with some apprehension the missions remaining in our tour of duty. Even the crew had lost some of its cockiness and its "we're hot stuff" attitude had given way to moody silence, as we were driven out to our ship before a raid.

Jack was our pilot and a darned good one, as well as a close friend of mine. Though we didn't talk about it, we knew that too many of the bomber crews that trained with us in New Mexico were being shot down. That knowledge made us realize how vulnerable we were. After Felner's plane was downed, a sense of foreboding seemed to be with us on every mission. His four officers had passed many an hour in our Nissan hut playing poker and pinochle. A certain camaraderie had developed and with their loss we began paying attention to details that had seemed only a bother before, even attached significance to every little event.

Prior to the Munich raid it seemed as if some invisible power was dictating our every move and giving us subtle clues on how to prepare ourselves for whatever was to come. Jack and I mailed home all of the souvenirs we had collected during three months of travel through South America, North Africa and the British Isles. There was no reason for our action, as duty was certain to keep us in England for several more months, but it was as though we wanted to leave no loose ends and were preparing for the worst. We were becoming a superstitious lot.

The day before the Munich raid, I took every stitch of my clothes into Norwich to be cleaned. It was usually my habit to leave behind any papers that might be of importance but, on the fateful day of this raid, I took the receipt with me. It was a trivial incident but an odd coincidence, rather like putting furniture in a warehouse, then throwing away any record that would link me as the owner. My clothes, no doubt, became the property of a grateful shopkeeper. What a shift in my usual habit of good planning.

That evening, after visiting the cleaners, I met with Bob Korth and Leo Carey, our navigator and bombardier, and went on a mild spree there in Norwich. It seemed almost like a carefree leave-taking of the status quo since, ordinarily, we saved our partying for "stand-down" nights. After a few drinks had lubricated the conversation at our table, a rather homely young English woman, who had joined us with her sister, confided that she was desperately in need of information. She went on to say that, in a moment of weakness, she allowed herself to be seduced by an American sergeant. When she later learned herself to be pregnant, he left her to her fate. "Oh," she said bitterly, "he fed me a line. You Yanks are good at that. I don't mean you, Luv. I wrote to him," she continued, "and pleaded with him to help me, but he never answered."

"Listen," she said as she clutched my arm, "could you find out what financial assistance, if any, I could get from the American government?" At that point, my senses were somewhat dulled, but such agitation as she displayed lent credence to her story and I began to feel sorry for her. Hastily, she scribbled her name and address on a scrap of paper and pressed it in my hand. I said that I would do whatever I could to help.

At any other time, I would have refused to become involved. With a clearer head, I would have been skeptical, rather than flattered, that she trusted me to get the information she wanted. She sighed with relief and her sister, who sat with us, said, "At last we have found a friend."

Later I thought, a stupid friend indeed. Norwich was full of eager young females. She could merely want my signature on a letter in order to build a case against me, naming me the father, hoping to extract money or marriage. With a clearer head, all sorts of scenarios played out in my mind but I had made a promise and wasn't given to going back on my word, even under such doubtful circumstances as these. As it turned out, Providence intervened. The unfortunate young woman was left with a promise I couldn't fulfill and I was saved from my own gullibility. Was this a benevolent act of providence in my behalf?

But those incidents before the Munich raid were relatively minor. There was the letter I was strangely prompted to write to my parents. I felt compelled to tell them that, if they should receive word that I was missing in action, they were not to give up hope and that they were to prepare Jeanne for the shock. My previous letters had all been cheerful and never dwelt on the negative, as I knew that anything else would only serve to reduce morale on the home front. But I had that feeling that something was going to happen.

There was a packet of letters from Jeanne awaiting me at the base, when we got back from Norwich. It was late and the party high was long gone. All I wanted to do was sleep. I started to toss them into my foot locker, but thought better of it when I remembered we had a mission to fly the next day. I sat on the edge of my bunk and read them one by one, each a link to home. Had I not read them then, I might not have had a second chance.

Another strange coincidence was the one concerning Jack Farmer's promotion. We had known that he was due for a First Lieutenant's commission, so Bob, Leo and I, his crew of officers, while we were in Norwich purchased as presents for him two sets of shiny silver bars. That night, when we returned to the base, Jack was asleep and we discovered by finding a brand new silver bar on one of his shirt collars that he had been promoted that very day. Since he had not yet changed the bars on his blouse, I pinned a new one on each shoulder and my own set of pilot wings over his left pocket, as a surprise for him. By a stroke of ill fate he was destined not to wear the blouse again for a very long time, if ever. That set of pilot wings, the same set that Jeanne pinned on me when I graduated from flying school, were never returned.

Probably the most significant incident of all was the loss of my cigarette lighter. Jeanne had given me a neat little Thorens lighter for my birthday just a year earlier. Its monetary value was negligible, but I attached a great deal of sentiment to it. It had accompanied me on every flight and it seemed like a little bit of Jeanne herself flying with me. Jack's Ronson and my Thorens were always on the control pedestal between us, where they travelled many thousands of miles. The compact efficiency of the Thorens never failed to elicit comment, as it nearly always lit with the first flick.

The Thorens was the last of three treasured gifts from Jeanne and losing it was almost like a mortal wound. The other two, my wedding ring and a camera, had been lost during some of my air force travels and I had taken their loss somewhat philosophically but the little lighter, which had been with me through the most adventurous year of my life, had become more than a cigarette lighter to me. It was a symbol of good luck and its loss left me with an empty feeling, almost as though I had been set adrift, a victim of the winds of fate with nothing to hang onto.

The feeling was so strong that I actually expected something to go wrong on the two missions that followed its loss. On returning from each mission, I searched the revetment where our ship was parked and tried to remember when it was last in my pocket. I felt sure that if I found it, everything would be alright again. During one of my searches, Jack stood and watched and finally said with disgust, "For God's sake, Toye, forget it. It's only a lighter. The world won't come to an end just because you lost it."

I had never been superstitious, but I was certainly acting like I was. It wasn't just a lighter. It seemed as though my life depended on it being in my possession. On this, the third mission since its loss, I fairly well expected that we were in for trouble.

B-24 Liberator production line
Photo courtesy of U.S. Air Force

The Liberator Bomber

Though they drank heavily and played hard, the American airmen in England were becoming both a religious and a superstitious lot. Some denounced all pleasures of the flesh and immersed themselves in Church and Bible tenets, hoping, in the event they didn't survive the conflict, they would have sufficiently atoned for any black marks and the gates of heaven would be opened to them. Some of the men in Jack Farmer's crew did a lot of praying at times and others put their faith in omens and good luck charms.

Jack hung from the cockpit ceiling a pair of miniature leather moccasins and a rabbit's foot. He always made sure they were there before we took off on a mission. I hadn't realized that my precious lighter served the same purpose until I lost it. Almost every man on the crew had a good luck charm, an old coin, a "giddy-giddy" from an African native, or some old keepsake that he felt would keep him from harm and bring him home safely. These beliefs were multiplied by every crew on the base.

Quite naturally then, on April 13, 1944, when we learned we were scheduled for a mission to Munich, the number 13 stood out with glaring clarity and was not exactly to our liking. When the huge wall map was uncovered, black and red strings strung between thumbtacks outlined our proposed route. The briefing room filled with excited oh's and ah's that always followed the announcement of a long mission. In the hush that followed, I heard someone say, as if he were trying to convince himself, "What if it is the 13th? It's only Thursday, not Friday. Hell, you aren't superstitious of an old number, are you?" I am sure that several others were happier that it was Thursday and not a Friday.

Captain Casey, briefing officer for the day, explained the raid. The marshalling yards and industrial area were the primary objectives. Although he didn't mention it, we had been told the night before that our old friend and former squadron C.O., Major James Stewart of motion picture fame, would be leading our wing. He had been transferred to our rival 453rd Group to fill a higher position, so we hadn't seen much of him for awhile, but we had faith in him. The raids Major Stewart led were always successful. That is to say, we found our targets, released our bombs with good effect and returned home safely. Regretfully, that was not always the case when other C.O.'s led our formation. It was a boost to think he would be with us on this one.

When the briefing was completed, we gathered in the "Ready Room" where we changed to our flight clothes. It was here that pre-flight tension began to mount. It was an almost palpable presence, affecting the men like football players before a big game.

Some unexplainable feeling caused me to put extra rations and cigarettes in my musette bag, as I had done ever since the loss of my lighter. We were told that our flight altitude would be colder than usual, so I donned a complete electrical suit and then tossed my G.I. shoes in the musette bag. They would be comfortable to walk in, in the event we had to bail out over Europe, and were said to closely resemble the shoes worn by farmers and other workers there. I made certain that each crew member had received his escape kit and there was an extra parachute and oxygen mask in case of failure or damage of one in flight. Sergeant Butler, the bottom Sperry turret gunner, joined me at my locker and said, "Here's the phone number to use to call for help in case we should have to escape to Switzerland."

I mulled over that information for a moment, thinking it strange that Butler should mention it now. We had been on raids near Switzerland several times and no one had bothered to give us the Legation phone number before. He was so impressed with information he confided, he had written it in ink on the back of his hand.

When we were dressed in warm flight clothes and all the various personal flying accessories were checked and accounted for, it was my job to assemble the crew to board the trucks waiting to take us to our ship. Jack and Bob remained behind to receive last minute pilot and navigator briefing.

Lennon, our radio operator, a Bostonian with an exaggerated accent, was not with us this morning. He had been hospitalized and unable to accompany us on other raids. This time there seemed to be some mystery attached to the fact that he hadn't reported for duty. The men didn't talk about it. We knew he was afraid. Most of us experienced some degree of fear, but that didn't make us cowards. I read someplace that the real heroes were the ones who were afraid but did what had to be done in spite of their fear.

Lennon had taken up radio because he thought it was a cushy job and felt it would somehow insulate him from the dangers the rest of us faced. After he had been on a few raids, he had a rude awakening and had actually voiced the intention of quitting or finding some way of being grounded. The men resented his attitude and felt he was the worst kind of gold bricker. There was a fierce loyalty among the crew members, kind of an obsession that they couldn't get along without each other and he was letting them down.

But Lennon felt no responsibility to the crew and preferred to be labeled the "Soap Box Orator." With little or no encouragement, he would bitch at great length about the shortcomings of the system, the state of the G.I. in general and himself in particular. Strangely, he felt some loyalty toward our ship. He even wrote an excellent essay endeavoring to gain recognition and respect for the Liberator as compared to the Flying Fortress, which enjoyed considerably more acclaim. He was writing thumbnail sketches of the crew members as related to them in combat. Perhaps the reason I tended to overlook his shortcomings more than the crew did, was because he had flattered me in his last article by saying that I was always calm under enemy fire and my voice over the intercom was cool and encouraging. He had no way of knowing that I purposely forced myself to speak in that way, not only to calm the men, but to convince myself that all was well. Roosevelt was right — the only thing we had to fear was fear itself, but in our case there was the flak and enemy planes to contend with.

My pumped up ego allowed me to forgive Lennon's absence but, with a strange member on the crew, I was uneasy. The substitute operator, whose name I can't remember, was a tall meek-looking fellow who was drafted from Torpey's old crew. Torpey was the pilot of a ship starting a mission the previous week. He saw two ships collide and explode in front of him as his formation accidently crossed the path of another during assembly. He returned to base in the thickest fog any of us had ever seen and requested that he be sent to a "flak home". On our first raid, a "Big B" raid to Berlin, we had a substitute for Lennon who turned out to be "flak happy." He sabotaged our radio so badly we were forced to abort. I didn't want this to happen again.

When our truck taxi let us out at the ship, I made it a point to talk to the new operator, hoping to satisfy myself that he was alright. He was an unusually quiet person, perhaps trying to reassure himself after learning of last week's disaster, but he seemed forthright, level headed and capable, and I relaxed a little as I busied myself with duties around the ship.

Our ship, number 132, or "Nine Yanks and a Jerk," as she had been lovingly christened by her original crew, was an old "H" model, for we had not earned the right to fly the later and more desirable "J" model. Nevertheless, she was a great pet of ours. We had flown four of our six missions with her. On the first one, with two engines crippled by flak, when it seemed certain we would go down in the Channel, she brought us back and landed us safely on English soil. That song, "Coming in on a Wing and a Prayer" could have been written about us. This was her thirtieth mission, the one that would complete our tour of the E.T.O., had we flown every mission with her. In those thirty missions she had not had a single abort. That was indeed an enviable record. Only one other ship on the base could claim such a record.

Our ground crew was also considered the best on the base. They often labored long past the usual working hours, giving every working part attention in order to keep our ship in tip top flying condition. On this April morning we found NYAAJ with a new set of heavy plexiglass windows armoring her cockpit. The ground crew worked all night to complete the job. She also had new rubber fittings for the number three and four engine superchargers. Jack and I had discovered on our last flight that they would not hold their pressure at high altitudes. The weary ground crew beamed their satisfaction with the job they had done. Jimmy, the crew chief, sagging with fatigue explained, "I've given 'er a ground test for the new fittings and she holds her pressure fine. I'd never let my boys quit a job on 'er until I was sure she was okay for the next run. I always say, 'Do the job right and she'll bring you fellas back okay.'"

I gave Jimmy the praise he expected and didn't voice my concern that only ground tests had been run. Superchargers rarely exhibited defects on the ground, but it was too late to do anything about it now.

"Seen anything of my lighter?" I asked.

"No, sir," he answered. "I'd sure tell you if we found it, 'cause I don't want nothin' that ain't mine." He always defended himself in this manner, sure that every officer thought the G.I.'s were thieves or worse.

I made my customary visual check of the outer surfaces and gear, making sure they were in good order and that the ground crew hadn't left any cowlings loose or parts lying around. For some reason I neglected to make my usual check of the oxygen bottles, a lapse that I was to later regret. On an earlier occasion, Jimmy was more than a little disgruntled when I insisted just a few minutes before flight time that he replace all ten bottles for some with full pressure.

Inspection completed, Jack and Bob came from the briefing room and we took our stations to check our individual equipment. During the engine warmup Jack and I tested numbers 3 and 4 superchargers, just for our own satisfaction. All instruments recorded perfect readings and we were ready to taxi out.

Our initial excitement levelled off when we learned by radio that take-off time had been moved back because of heavy early morning fog. It wasn't until a few minutes before ten that we received the signal for all clear to begin our assembly. The "Zebra," a sort of bell weather ship with her orange and black stripes, began her lumbering taxi to the head of the runway. As her motors revved up, our tension and excitement built with the sound. It was the "Zebra's" job to act as Queen Bee for her flock of Libs and gather them into formation over the field. Her stripes, her special lighting equipment to be used when necessary and the fixing of colored flares from her lead position helped to guide us into formation. Jack taxied in about the fifth position on the field perimeter track. We were flying a good position in the formation today, one that made us feel considerably more relaxed than the "Tail-end-Charley" position or "Coffin Corner" we had flown on the six previous missions.

On the perimeter track across the field from us, many more Libs taxied parallel to us, so that two lines could alternately feed ships into take-off position. One of the last remaining pilots from our old Alamagordo training days, Lt. Frasch, taxied directly in front of us. We saw that he was having trouble with his heavily laden ship. It kept rising off its nose wheel and teetering on the main gear until the tail strut came down on the pavement with a bang. It reminded me of a mule balking in the traces and refusing to pull a heavy load.

We finally moved along smoothly past the ground personnel who turned out in force to watch this late take-off. Jack and I practically sat at attention with our elbows resting on the side windows, as we acknowledged the V for victory signs flashed our way, feeling like heroes riding in a parade.

"Those guys turned out to write our epitaph," Jack shouted above the roar of the engines. There might have been some truth in what he said. We often thought the spectators turned out because they were looking for a cheap thrill such as a crash on take-off or, in the event we didn't come back, they could say they were the last to see us. Really not much better than the spectators at a bull fight—a sad commentary on human nature.

These few minutes before the "Zero hour" were always filled with apprehension and fear of what lay ahead. This truth was confessed by many men of bomber crews as well as fighter pilots, and I was not one to deny it. Once the flight had begun, all attention was riveted on fulfilling the functions in which we had trained, squelching any further thoughts of fear. Anything less would have been an invitation to violate the natural law of self preservation. But in these few minutes before take-off, not even a spurt in the drone of the idling engines could break the revery in which each man found himself thinking of the things that made life precious—home, family, country...

In these long taxiing lines each Lib suddenly took on the personality of an individual and the ten men inside, made of flesh and blood and possessing a man's five senses, now became its internal organs. The crew collectively comprised the muscles, the heart and the brain of this ugly monster, ungainly on the ground, but once in the air, responsive and dependable. Each man thought of himself as the single motivating force for his airplane. On a Munich raid there was no doubt that some of the ships would return crippled and others would not return at all. But each man considered it practically an impossibility that fate would select his ship for an ugly demise, but should it happen, certainly he himself would survive, regardless of what happened to the rest of the crew. Actually, that philosophy was a sort of defense mechanism; it served to protect us from the unthinkable.

At exactly 1,000 hours the Zebra pulled slowly down the mile long runway with engines roaring in loud unison. Before reaching the half way point, she began to rise effortlessly, for she carried no heavy bomb load like her sisters. Her job would be completed when she had assembled her sister ships over a designated area. The signalman in the black and white control truck flashed a green light on his altus lamp and another big ship roared down the runway, this time using almost the entire mile before getting off with its heavy bombload.

As we moved up in line toward the take-off point, I made my customary checks, set the rich fuel mixture and toggled the cowl flaps in trail. We were carrying 5,000 pounds of small fragment bombs in clusters, a load more ticklish to handle than one of 500 or 1,000 pound G.P.'s. Jack checked his controls, gave last second orders to the engineer and we waited for the green light. "All set?" he called to me.

"Okay here."

There was the green light! Jack held on his brakes as he revved up all the engines at once to give us the extra pull needed to get our heavy load rolling. "Nine Yanks and a Jerk" responded by straining like a greyhound on leash. There was no more time to think of life's precious moments, only time to be alert and do the job we had been trained to do.

Over Munich

As Jack released his pressure on the brake pedals, the overweighted Lib shuddered for a split second before beginning its roll down the runway. Under his expert guidance, it took a straight course along the center line, laboriously gathering speed in every second. A barn and trees at the end of the runway rushed up to meet us, but Jack held his ship down to use the entire one mile length. We had to gain the greatest possible speed in order to become airborne without the danger of stalling. Jack was one of the best to perform this critical function. When the end of the runway was almost under us, he pulled back on the control column and the Lib struggled mightily to free itself of the ground. We were airborne!

Even though the takeoff noise of the engines was deafening, it was music to the pilot's and copilot's ears. Anything less could indicate imminent engine failure. England's green landscapes rushed under us at a terrific pace. It seemed we could almost reach out and touch the tree tops. A crucial point of every flight, it was necessary that every engine function perfectly, for if any one of them faltered, we could not remain airborne. Furthermore, we wouldn't have attained sufficient altitude for the crew to bail out.

"Gear up," came Jack's crisp command to Standridge, our flight engineer, a few seconds after we had taken off.

"Forty-five, twenty-five," he directed at me. The number indicated the manifold pressure and R.P.M. setting he wanted me to give him.

"Forty-three, twenty-four, fifty." This command for me from Jack usually followed Standridge's announcement that the gear was up.

"Flaps up," Jack directed at me again when we had gained sufficient speed.

"Forty-one, twenty-four." Generally, this would be his last command during these first tense moments. We truly flew by the numbers. No other commands were needed. Every man knew his job well enough. Standridge transferred fuel from the auxiliary to the main tanks; the radio operator tuned his set; I performed minor adjustments to keep my engine instruments reading accurately, while Bob and Leo, our navigator and bombardier, took their positions in the nose. Objects on the ground were becoming smaller and the initial tension was easing. It was a good time for a cigarette, if we could get one in before Standridge started his fuel transfer.

The skies over East Anglia were filled with the usual haze. Oftentimes, it reached such density that other ships were barely visible and there were many near collisions. Everywhere we looked, East Anglia's American bases had filled the air with Libs and Forts, some flying in straggly disorder as they attempted their assembly. Most of them wandered in search of their own group. The Zebras fired colored flares, signalling ships of their own bases to join them.

We spotted our own red and green and flew through the maze of ships to get into our own area. We crossed the paths of untold numbers of these bombers still searching for their own group. The sky in this case had definite limits and it necessitated a system of grids in an attempt to prevent absolute chaos. Order was accomplished by a "buncher" system which was a series of radio control stations. In each station a quadrangle of four radio towers sent out a signal on an assigned frequency which was picked up by the airplane radio compass. A fifth tower in the center of the quadrangle indicated to the pilot by a light signal on his instrument panel when he was directly over the station. There were as many of these stations as could be fitted into the limited sky space of East Anglia.

Our Libs, with big capital letter "F"s in black on a white circle painted on the outer surface of each vertical stabilizer, were now into some semblance of flight order. Our Zebra directed us in a wide circle around "buncher six," enabling ships attempting to join the formation to cut across the circle and quickly close up the distance.

A large flight of Forts forming on "buncher five" in the opposite direction converged on us. The two Zebras banked sharply to their inside to tighten their circles and avoid collisions. That wasn't enough, however, and our Libs in the rear circling wide passed squarely into the center of the Fort formation.

"Those sons-of-bitches," I yelled as I signaled Jack to let me take over. The copilot's seat afforded a better view of what was befalling us. The oath fell on deaf ears but it served to vent my feelings. We avoided disaster and the tense moments passed. I stayed on the controls, as Jack preferred to take over when we were deep in enemy territory, leaving me to do the flying under less dangerous conditions. When we reached 10,000 feet altitude, I leveled off to wait for the rest of our ships to join the group. I relayed the information to the crew over the interphone and added, "I'll let you know when we start climbing again." This was the last chance for the boys to get a cigarette before we climbed to the level where oxygen was needed. By now, the three turrets and two waist guns had been checked for mobility and radio intercom but had not yet test fired.

Our group had shaped up into an impressive and seemingly invincible formation, the two lead elements nicely boxed together. From our vantage point looking into the sun, the six ships ahead of us looked like evenly spaced sticks flying broadside through the air. Frasch was leading the fourth element and we flew number two position off his right wing. We were so close we could see Frasch's gunners grinning from their waist windows, as they mocked our gunners. The spirit of the raid was upon us now.

Our Zebra continued to circle us over buncher six for nearly two hours. A police ship from our base zipped in and around our formation taking pictures to be used later in briefings or as a means for critique.

At the exact moment the assembly was scheduled to be completed, our Zebra turned away from buncher six and led us in the direction of another radio controlled area designated "splasher six." There we formed a wing composed of three groups. Timing was critical, as perfect coordination of the raid depended on it. There were to be several wing formations that would move out together, several hundred planes in all. By now the sun had dissipated haze and we could see the waters of the Channel shimmering below us. At our altitude it looked as cold and flat as slate.

Our Zebra tied us in behind the 453rd led by Major Stewart, then left us on our own. The 389th moved in from high on our right to complete Major Stewart's wing. Other wings were already formed ahead of us and bombers flew in close formation for as far as we could see.

This massive armada was so impressive that only those participating could fully appreciate the magnitude of what was happening. We swelled with pride at the sight of the flotilla of ships visible in every direction. Although the purpose of the raid was known to us, we detached ourselves from the knowledge that the bombs we dropped would also bring, not just destruction, but death to hundreds of civilians unable to comprehend why we rent our vengeance on them. It was our job, something someone else had started, men with positions of power who supposedly knew more than we did. We were but the implements of war, although at this moment we were proud to be part of the tremendous strength of our country.

With this vast death parcel heading for Munich, turrets began to swing and machine guns to spat angrily, as gunners tested their equipment. Beckham, our tail gunner and Butler, the bottom turret gunner, were crammed into their tight quarters and Standridge climbed into the turret overhead. The two waist guns were handled by Suber and Kerpan. Yellow flares from our group leader signaled us to begin our climb to 20,000 feet. At that altitude we could escape most of the flak that towns on the European coastline would throw at us, as well as to be at our bombing target level.

Jack increased power for me and I called all stations to put on their masks. Wing formations ahead of us had already begun their climb and were stairstepped into the morning sun. Soon the flat unimpressive shores of Belgium stretched out before us, and we began to prepare for whatever dangers lurked there.

"Co-pilot to radio. Co-pilot to radio. Give us our flak suits and helmets." Jack and I always waited until this point, because our work was strenuous and the bulky vests hampered our movements.

"Pilot to all stations. Pilot to all stations. Report all unidentified aircraft in the vicinity."

"Fighters at three o'clock," came a voice from one station, probably Talmadge Suber's in the right waist position, alerting gun stations for possible enemy attack. The fighters turned out to be our own P-47 Thunderbolts rendezvousing with us to serve as our fighter escort. They were always a welcome sight. By this time, crew members were beginning to feel more vulnerable and the fighters were added insurance in case of attack.

It was my job to monitor the V.H.F. (very high frequency) radio as well as our interphones, in case of any change of plan by our leader. These commands rarely came through, as it was considered more important to maintain radio silence over enemy territory. While I listened in, I heard an exchange about an English Spitfire that had gone down in flames somewhere ahead of us. The battle was already on and our turn would come soon.

"Light flak at two o'clock," came a voice through the intercom. Puffs of angry black smoke to the right indicated that Brussels was sending us her usual greeting card. It was random firing, giving us notice that we couldn't pass over the city unchallenged.

"Unidentified aircraft at two o'clock low," came a report from one of our stations. These turned out to be Forts returning or aborting from a raid that preceded ours. I counted nine, a much greater number than usual. I calculated that, if they really were aborts, their raid must have had tough going.

At our flight level, the sun was shining bright, but below us scattered cumulus clouds had moved over the continent. Wherever there were breaks, we could see the neat, pale green squares of farmers' fields, the red tile of roofs and the dark green patches of forests. The sun's rays, magnified as they filtered through the plexiglass windows, brought a welcome warmth to our blood and the peaceful scenes below belied reality, lulling us for a moment away from the need for alertness over enemy territory. Liege was off to our right, but all was quiet and a few minutes later we crossed the border into "old" Germany.

Our routes over Europe were always planned to avoid the worst flak areas, so we passed to the South of Koblenz, the southernmost town in the Ruhr Valley which our boys had nicknamed "Flak Alley." Bob, our navigator, from his nose position spotted what appeared to be the construction of new

Nazi defenses against the expected invasion. The few airdromes we passed over seemed lifeless. There were no planes and the strips were pock-marked from the continuous pounding they took from the R.A.F. and our boys. We turned a few degrees South, as we neared Ludswighafen and proceeded in a direct line toward Lake Constance, avoiding the flak at Stuttgart and Karlsruhe.

Our P-47 Thunderbolt escort passed us on to a group of P-51 Mustangs. Their limited gas supply wouldn't permit them to stay with us the whole way. There was always a lapse of time when one group left and before the second took over. It was then we felt naked and alone. We knew that our own guns were not enough to hold off the desperate German fighter planes. We had no illusions about their ability to do a job on us. Pilot, co-pilot and navigator felt particularly helpless, because we didn't have guns for support, something that would at least give us the feeling we were doing something to help ourselves. At this point, Jack took over the controls.

As we neared Lake Constance, our leader discovered we were a couple minutes ahead of schedule. He S'd the formation so we wouldn't override other wings bombing the same target. At Lake Constance we turned left almost ninety degrees to a northeasterly direction and paralleled the Alps for about fifty miles. The next turn to the left was at the Wing I.P. (initial point) and would take us directly over the target at Munich.

Before we reached the I.P., I saw three ships turn off in formation with all fans turning and head for Switzerland. There had been assertions that there were instances of desertions like this before, but these three could have been hit by flak or possibly experienced engine troubles along the way. In any case, I silently wished them luck and then focused back on our own problems.

Red flares from the lead ship signaled that we had reached the Wing I.P. and we turned back West toward our target.

There would no doubt be heavy flak coming up from such a well-defended city as Munich, but the groups ahead of us were not yet encountering any. Bob called over the interphone that we were right on target. "Bomb bay doors open," Jack called to the radio operator, following the signal given by the opening of doors ahead.

Leo came out of the nose turret and made last minute inspection of his release switches. One flick of his finger would send destruction raining down on the Munich railroad yards. I strained to catch some conversation that was going on between Leo and Bob. It concerned the bomb release, but Leo was one of those who had never learned to enunciate clearly over the interphone.

The scene below seemed as peaceful as had the Belgium countryside. The drone of the engines was all that filled our ears, giving us a false sense of security. The flatness of the city, the lack of imposing structures gave no hint that anti-aircraft emplacements could be hidden there. It appeared simple; all we had to do was go over the target, drop our load and head for home. I had halfway come to the belief that the intense opposition we had met on earlier raids over industrial centers near the coast meant that Germany's inland cities had been stripped of all defenses. Not one puff of ack-ack had yet appeared.

Suddenly, the peaceful illusion was shattered. In the back of my mind I knew it couldn't last. The vast expanse of sky that seemed to protect us suddenly became so mottled with angry little black puffs of ack-ack, so close together it seemed I could step out and walk from one to another. It wasn't just a small box barrage like we had seen at other times; it was spread out in heavy concentration over at least a twenty mile square. It was designed to intercept our formation in every quarter of the city. The fire was deadly accurate and formed a black curtain right at our level. Our planes were so close together that there was no room for evasive action, action that we couldn't take anyway, now that we were heading in on the target. Those Jerries were cagey and held their fire until they had us trapped.

Even rows of bursts were all around us now and I could predict by the equidistant spacing of puffs just where the six in each series would pin point. One row of six commenced close to our wing on my side and converged toward the nose where Leo tensely waited for the bombs away signal. "Three, four, five," I counted. "Oh, my God, the sixth should explode right under our nose." I braced myself but there was no sound. Our nose entered the middle of the black blob of smoke and scattered it into silky wisps. It missed! A tight squeak if there ever was one.

"Get us out of this God-awful stuff," Jack shouted loud enough for me to hear, even though his mike button was turned off. His wasted epithet was directed at our leader. The roar of our engines masked the sound of the explosions, but we knew well enough that what appeared to be harmless smoke blobs were filled with deadly shrapnel.

We were accustomed to loosening up the formation just before the target to clear each ship for its bomb drop and now the widened gaps between us saved our lives. Frasch's ship took a direct hit in the fuselage. It collapsed into chunks in the midsection as if it had been a kid's wooden toy being crushed by a boulder. A big hunk of tail section flew in our direction and the ship cartwheeled lifelessly as it dived earthward out of sight. This happened without a sound reaching our ears. Jack and I pulled up hard on the dual controls to get us over the flying debris.

Still only the steady drone of our engines filled our ears. It was our eyes that had to tell us of the terrific battle going on around us. It was impossible to grasp the reality that ten men had very possibly lost their lives in that explosion. We were more used to thinking of the planes around us as mere machines, not as containers holding ten flesh and blood men inside. At least several of our men had seen this terrible thing happen, but not a sound came over the interphone attesting it. Our voices were stifled with expectancy, awe and fear.

"Three parachutes at six o'clock low," came a quiet announcement. That had to be Beckham, our tail gunner. He wouldn't have seen the explosion from his tail position and couldn't know that the three parachutes just might be carrying corpses of some of Frasch's men blown out of the midsection. Reason told me that if any of them were alive, they had probably escaped from the waist. Men in the nose would more likely be trapped by the downward momentum as the ship spun earthward. I knew Frasch well and would like to have believed he was alive, but it seemed doubtful.

Beckham's voice had broken the spell that held us in silence. Suddenly, everyone was trying to talk over the interphone at once. We had passed over the dangerous flak area safely and reaction now set in. "That was the worst yet," Jack said shakily, as he exhaled in relief. No comment was necessary. We all shared the same sentiment.

"Why the hell didn't we drop our bombs?" Leo was asked. Down there in his nose compartment, he didn't know the answer any more than the rest of us. Pattern bombing was only a matter of the bombardier pressing the release switch when he saw "bombs away" in the ship ahead. While we were passing through that living hell, we had been frozen in time and had passed over the target without realizing it. No ship ahead of ours had released its bombs. In spite of that, our spirits began to rise as we congratulated ourselves on our survival.

"Where is that damn fighter escort?" Jack called out exasperatedly. "They're never around when you want them." He was always first to sense a new danger. His question stifled the premature high hopes of the crew and put them back on the lookout for an enemy even more formidable than flak.

I increased my own vigilance to detect any of those vicious German wasps with the deadly sting. At the same time, I began to realize that something had happened to our formation and was still happening. One ship below and to the left of us had a patch of flame coming through the top of its left wing. A ship ahead of us was trailing black smoke from its number two engine. The flak had taken its toll and I knew there could be even more damage before it was over.

The action also had a demoralizing effect on our bombing formation. With little regard for order in keeping a tight defense, ships were hunting better positions to give wider berth for ships smoking or burning or to fill the open space left by the loss of a ship. Also formations had unconsciously overridden one another while going over the target. We were like a football team without a quarterback. One wing that had been behind us was now abreast of us with part of its ships just below ours. Ships from another wing, originally flying a high right position behind us, had now overtaken us and were crossing overhead. One of its Libs, evidently unaware that we were below, opened its bomb bay doors. I watched in unbelieving horror, as I realized what was about to happen and I galvanized into action. "Let me have it a minute, Jack. This joker above us is about to drop his bombs." Without waiting for a reply, I took the controls and eased us into the vacancy left by Frasch's missing ship. It put us out from underneath, just as the bombs began pouring from the Lib's belly above us.

"That dirty bastard!" Jack cursed, as the bombs dropped a hundred yards off our right wing tip. "Get his number, Don. I'm going to turn him in when we get back."

Jack took over and moved us back into our original position and away from the Lib with the burning wing, which had somehow passed under us during the excitement. We knew it could explode at any second. The ships overhead had cleared.

We began to breathe more easily but it wasn't to last long. "We'd better salvo these damn bombs," Bob called on the interphone.

Since we were still behind German borders, Jack considered it a wise move and we began looking below, hoping to pass over a likely target. Before finding one, however, we encountered a new threat.

"Fighters at five o'clock low," came the unwelcome announcement from Suber, one of our waist gunners, in his quiet Georgia drawl. That voice came through as if it belonged to somebody in grade school, rather than from a man holding onto a machine gun in a ferocious battle. The little boy sounds were still echoing in my ears when suddenly all hell broke loose. A loud explosion sounded aft of the pilot's compartment. The ship shuddered and dipped with its forward progress momentarily interrupted, as if it was uncertain whether to fly or drop out of the sky. As the Lib quavered hesitantly, it was obvious from the sound's intensity that a missile considerably more powerful than a 50 calibre bullet, probably a 50 mm cannon shell, had slammed into us. The crashing sound had come from either the waist or tail section. With such a jolt as that, it was almost certain we'd have injuries and serious damage.

Bail Out!

Jack and I combined efforts to regain control. At the same time I began scanning the instruments for some indication of damage. Readings were normal. The props turned smoothly with no out of sync engine sound. When we found the ship would still fly, we waited for voices to indicate the seat of the damage and the extent of the injuries.

"Salvo the bombs," Jack ordered sharply.

"Bombs away," came Leo's shaky response to the order. We weren't concerned now about what we might hit. Our thoughts were focused on the damage to our ship. When no voices from behind came on the interphone, I began to envision us flying along with nothing but a nose section attached to the wings. Had everyone been killed?

"Co-pilot to waist! Co-pilot to waist!" I called, but there was no answer.

Suddenly Suber's boyish voice broke the silence. "We've been hit back here by a twenty millimeter. Beckham is hurt." His voice was well modulated without any hysteria.

Joe Kerpan, the waist gunner repeated with a gasp, "Yeah, we've been hit. Looks pretty bad." He didn't release the mike button and his frantic sobbing filled us with apprehension of what other horrors the shell had wrought in the waist section.

Foolishly we ignored any further possibility of enemy fighters, since we were now more concerned with our men's injuries and the condition of the ship. I began questioning Suber, trying to assess the damage. "How bad is Beckham hurt?"

"He's bleeding around the face but I guess he's alright," Suber answered in a voice still well controlled.

"Are you and Joe okay?" I queried.

"Joe's alright. I got hit in the leg but it's not bad. I'll be okay."

"Can one of you take over the tail guns?"

"Beckham's coming out now. I'll ask him. I think the tail turret was knocked out." Suber was the only one in the waist who seemed capable of answering my questions.

"OK," I answered him. I'll be back in a minute to give you some first aid."

Suddenly Beckham's voice broke in, "The tail turret is knocked out and we've got a big hole back here." His voice was quiet and steady. "I got a Messerschmitt," he added almost matter-of-fact. His mention of the Messerschmitt interested me more for the moment than did an account of the damage. After all, we still had control of the ship. "Did anyone see him go down?" I asked excitedly. This was our first score and we needed confirmation by another party in order to get credit for the kill.

"That's right. I saw him go down in flames," Suber confirmed. His voice was casual. His focus just now was on the mass of destruction in the waist and he didn't seem much interested in a downed Me 109.

Beckham broke in, "I tried to tie up the cables back here, but some of them are frayed too bad. I got all I could." That was the first knowledge we had of cable damage.

"We still have control up here," I countered. Probably only one of the dual sets had been shot out, I surmised.

"Co-pilot to Butler. Are you O.K.?"

"I'm fit as a fiddle," Butler replied flippantly, in an attempt at nonchalance. Ordinarily he was a talkative kid, but he had kept amazingly quiet through all this.

"Co-pilot to Martin turret. You O.K.?"

"I'm O.K.," Standridge answered in his clear slow voice. He never appeared to be rattled, but Jack and I had learned after some previous scrapes that he had been pretty shook up. He was just good at hiding it.

During all this interchange, Jack had his hands full flying close formation and was content to just listen in, as I went about the business of gathering damage information. We had worked together longer than most pilots and co-pilots. I had been accustomed to relieving him of responsibilities other than piloting. He trusted me completely. Suber broke in, "How's your oxygen up there?"

"Mine's alright. Pressure 250," I answered.

"Mine's down to 100," he said, his voice still controlled. "I think our oxygen system was hit."

I immediately called the radio operator to take the boys our portables. But here I discovered the two behind the pilot seats were empty. Oh my God! My oversight had caught up with me under the worst possible conditions. "Have you got any bottles back there?" I asked.

"I think there's a couple and I still have a little pressure," Suber answered.

Joe Kerpan broke in, still gasping. "Yeah, mine's down too." Again he failed to release the mike button. It sounded as if he were crying. Suddenly he spat out a string of oaths, "I'll get the son-of-a-bitch." His guns started rattling. I feared for the worst, but nothing happened.

Suber's voice, for the first time revealing any excitement, cleared up the matter. "Hey Joe, that's a Mustang." Joe had mistaken it for an Me 109. Fortunately he missed.

"How much oxygen pressure have you now, Suber?"

"About 75 pounds."

"Let me know when it reaches 50 and we'll go down," I told him. We were still in formation and well into enemy territory. It would be a long chance, trying to make it back alone but we would have to take it. Our situation was going from bad to worse.

"Hey, number one engine is on fire," Joe shouted into the interphone. The ugly announcement shook me into the reality that our flight could be doomed. Up until now I felt sure we would make it back across the channel and had even let my thoughts idly picture the fuss that would be made over us when we told them our stories. Now my hopes were dimmed and I began thinking about parachuting over enemy territory. Jack and I leaned toward his window, where we craned our necks trying to see the fire. The wing's trailing edge, where it was bound to be, was obscure from our vision.

"It's pretty bad," Joe said, the urgency of the situation evident in his voice.

"Standridge, cut the fuel," Jack ordered.

I feathered the engine at Jack's command. After losing power from the number one engine, it took both of us to hold right rudder in an attempt to keep the ship on a straight course. That was when we discovered that it was the trim tab cables that had been shot out in back. Physical endurance was needed in their place. Once the engine was shut down, I tried to confine the fire in the nacelle by closing the cowl flaps and hoped the concentrated air stream would blow it out. Whether or not this was correct procedure as outlined in Air Corps manuals, it seemed to help.

"It's out now," Joe called, "but it's smoking pretty bad."

"Keep an eye on it, Joe and let us know if it flares up again," advised Jack.

"Now the tire is on fire," Joe yelled urgently. Jack ordered Bob and Leo out of the nose so he could lower the gear into the slipstream, but they said they'd just go further up into the nose. They wanted to be in position to jump, if Jack gave the order. The wind blew the fire out and Jack raised the gear again.

"Oh, oh, the fire has started in the wing again and it's bad," Joe exclaimed.

Bail Out!

The jig was up. It was plain there was nothing more we could do. We had to bail out before the fire reached the fuel tanks and the ship exploded. It still seemed unreal, as though we were mere spectators watching it all happen in a slow motion movie and could get up and walk out anytime. When it happened to other people, I had not been very disturbed, but what was happening now was real and personal, not something out of a story book.

"Pilot to all stations. Pilot to all stations. Bail out at once!" There was a finality in the words. The time had come. This eventuality is what we had bandied about so lightly in barracks bull sessions. In my dazed reaction to Jack's words, I echoed his command.

"Yeah, get going men!" I didn't know why I said it, other than to emphasize that there was no other recourse.

Bob's information that we were 150 miles from the Channel was one of the last remarks over the interphone. The very last one I remember was "Here I go" in Suber's quiet announcement. Although I called the other stations, I got no answer. We assumed that everyone had bailed out, for Suber would have waited until last. I called the nose but neither Bob or Leo answered. I then pressed the emergency bell as the final alarm.

Behind me I could see Standridge and the radio man sitting on the edge of the command deck, facing the open bomb bays. It appeared they were working with their chutes, evidently figuring they were safe until Jack and I left our seats. At first I considered waiting for them, thinking they might have some reason for not jumping. I had been helping Jack hold right rudder. When Jack looked at me inquiringly, I knew that he felt that it was urgent that I get going. I tossed my headgear aside, slipped out of my seat, grabbed my musette bag from behind it and lurched toward the bomb bays. By the time I got there, the two men had jumped. In the time it would take Jack to reach me, I intended to fasten the musette bag to me and thought he and I would jump together. But the ship shuddered violently and fell off to the left in a flat spin. That must have been when Jack took his foot off the rudder pedal. Without looking behind me, I held the musette bag in the crook of my arm and jumped. At that instant the ship exploded and I was thrown against the center girders.

My head banged against the bomb bay catwalk as I dropped through, then on the side of the ship. That was the last thing I remember clearly. I had a vague sensation of falling through a big red ball of fire. It seemed two flaming sections and many small pieces fell around me. This sensation was later confirmed for me to be true, since the left wing had blown off completely.

In something of a daze, I pulled the rip cord, but I seemed to fall endlessly. Although conscious enough of the falling debris to pray that it wouldn't slice me in two, I felt sure that it had, when my body took a terrific jolt that nearly tore my limbs from their sockets. Once more I was knocked into a semi-conscious state. In what must have been just a few seconds, I awoke to a ghastly silence. There was no sound of engines and no debris. Instead I was enveloped in a heavy mist and snow was flying upward into my face. In my battered and confused condition, I thought dreamily how silly it seemed that snow should be falling up instead of down. Then my head cleared and I realized I was in a cloud.

The iron chute handle was loose in my hand. Was it supposed to be that way? I couldn't remember. I must have had a death grip on it. A terrible fear gripped me that my chute might not have opened or that the shock I had received, supposedly from the flying debris, had severed one of my legs or an arm. I glanced cautiously, first above me to discover gloriously that a great expanse of silk was umbrellaed there and then at my arms and legs, which fortunately were intact. It was easy to conclude that the terrific shock had been from the parachute opening. A loud explosion off in the distance announced to me that our ship had at last crashed into the ground.

I began to take a more complete inventory of my injuries. I felt of my face, arms and legs, then looked closely at my hands. I had some minor bruises on my head and face. I had lost a slipper and overshoe from one foot and I looked with amazement at my mittens. One finger had been sheared off as neatly as if it had been cut by scissors, but my finger was still intact.

My groin hurt me most of all and I recalled with horror the tales I had heard of some airmen being castrated by improperly adjusted chutes. I moved my hands gingerly across my abdomen; it was okay but I had to keep pulling myself up in the harness to relieve the pain. What bothered me most was the musette bag. It must have been torn from my grip when I was blown out of the ship. I was going to set down in enemy territory without shoes or food rations and, worst of all, without a map, compass or money for escape.

These thoughts went through my mind, but were overridden by the knowledge that I had miraculously escaped almost certain death and only by the merest fraction of a second. In my semi-conscious state I could have pulled the ripcord prematurely and become entangled with some part of the plane. The flying debris could have sliced me in two or burned my parachute. Even the fact that the chute opened was a victory over chance. There were more than just a few cases where they hadn't. I was indeed lucky to be alive. I wondered if Jack made it. It didn't seem probable that he had. That would be an even greater miracle. There hadn't been time enough.

I moved down through the clouds, my chute swinging me in wide arcs as the wind caught it. It was an enjoyable sensation, but glimpses of the checkered green fields below reminded me that all was not yet well. Soon I would be with those little people down there, those people who were our enemies. Would I be taken prisoner? Would they shoot me as

I hung helpless in my chute? I had heard that they sometimes did. Would I break my legs in the fall? Everything seemed so abstract up here, with no sound but the rustle of the wind in my chute, no sight of human life down there on the ground. I was still about 5000 feet up.

Off in the distance, near one of those villages with the many red roofs, our Lib burned furiously, sending up a great billowing cloud of black smoke. The wind seemed to carry me purposefully away from the scene of the crash, as if to deposit me in a safer place. I looked around, hoping to see the chutes of all of my comrades. I counted seven. Assuming that Jack had not made it, there should still be one more to account for our full complement of ten. It was possible someone had not pulled his rip cord until he was close to the ground, as we had been briefed to do. In that case he could already be on the ground and concealed in the trees.

I was descending toward the smaller of two wooded areas that were identifiable by their much darker green. They would offer concealment, I thought. Desperately I tried to steer myself in their direction by tugging on the harness, but only succeeded in spilling the chute. After letting me plummet earthward like a shot for a second, my chute reopened and carried me over the top of the larger wood. It was certain now that I would land in between the two.

As the ground came up to meet me, I again tried to face downwind, so I would be in the direction for mobility when I landed. But I was falling faster than I had calculated and, before I could complete the maneuver, I hit the ground so hard that again I was momentarily stunned. Sitting up, I cautiously moved my legs. Although one knee had taken a terrific shock, I assumed that no bones were broken. Once again I was lucky.

Before I landed I had seen one of our group land close to a farmer plowing his field. Still another was swept into the larger of the two woods. My first impulse was to join this second man, but in my blind anxiety to find the nearest concealment, I gathered up my chute and fled into the smaller wood. This was a mistake, for the smaller wood turned out to be man made, one planted in even rows. There was no underbrush to offer concealment and I could be seen by anyone walking the perimeter. Nevertheless, I continued to flee from the spot of my fall deeper and deeper into this small wood in hopes of finding cover. It seemed hopeless. I was trapped, for on all sides were open fields. Finally in resignation I sat down to collect my thoughts. I hadn't the slightest idea of where I was and had no compass to guide me toward France, where I might possibly find a partisan group. Soon the Germans would arrive and I would be taken prisoner.

I hadn't much more than sat down when I heard someone running toward me. Trying to hide was out of the question, so I waited, heart pounding and raised my hands in surrender as three men approached. They appeared to be unarmed peasants, hardly the angered Germans I had expected. Instead of trying to overpower me, they ran toward me, grinning and gesturing like little children. They grasped my hand and shook it mightily, while all three talked at once. "Comrade, comrade, Lutsebush, Lutsebush!"

Amazement and relief flooded over me. They were plainly here as my friends, but what was this Lutsebush? They spoke in a language that didn't sound like German. One of them noticed my puzzled expression and slowly pronounced "Luxemburg, Luxemburg!"

That set me right at once. These were partisans of tiny Luxembourg. Bob had been wrong in his calculations, for Luxembourg is nearer 100 miles from the Channel than 150. I was stupefied with relief and returned their greetings. As my mind struggled to process all that had happened, my legs would no longer support me when the adrenalin subsided. I had to sit down. In a matter of minutes I had missed being hit by shrapnel, survived an explosion, missed being wiped out by debris, escaped the dangers of parachuting, and now in German territory landed in the hands of friends who would shelter me and show me the way to escape. What other series of events could better be called a set of miracles?

Rescue

I was impressed by one of my rescuers, mainly because of his remarkable resemblance to a fellow who had once worked in my father's machine shop. He had bright blue eyes under bushy eyebrows and a very large nose. A ruddy complexion and huge hands completed the picture. The other two would have made a good Laurel and Hardy team, one skinny and the other fat. They were red faced and perspiring with excitement.

Once the greetings were over, the Laurel and Hardy team jumped around like a couple of marionettes and began gesturing in a fashion that I guessed was their idea of a Chicago gangster or an American cowboy, while with intense but muted voices they kept saying "Mitrailleuses! mitrailleuses!"; then they would imitate the rat-tat-tat of machine guns.

This action at first seemed quite comical but I couldn't understand what they were trying to tell me. The big man pointed to my clothes, then to the parachute. The little man watched intently and then, like a Hollywood yes man, frantically imitated every motion. It finally dawned on me, they thought I was part of an invasion force and would have guns for them. When I shook my head, they looked frustrated and disappointed. I halfway expected them to abandon me to my fate. The little man watched his partner frisk my pockets, then he tore into my parachute, looking for something of value. He found the pocket of dye on my Mae West, the stuff that would show up in the water, if we had to bail out over the Channel. He ripped open the seams and was completely nonplussed when a great quantity of the yellow powdered dye spurted out on his hands and clothes. He turned to his boss with a "what do we do now?" look. The boss was plainly disgusted and motioned that it was time to get going. I thought it might be money they were after but couldn't make them understand that I had none. Once again, I yearned for the musette bag that had slipped from my grasp and hoped that some lucky finder could make use of its contents. The Laurel and Hardy team, after one more exuberant session of hand shaking with me, were off again as hurriedly as they had come.

My first rescuer, who had stood quietly by during all this, looked at me dejectedly. I was a problem; what was he to do with me? After he concealed the chute in the branches of a tree, he motioned for me to follow him. We went to the edge of the wood and scanned the fields for enemy patrols, which would certainly be alert after such a terrific air battle. At his urging we dashed across the open space and through a marsh. My one bare foot kept sinking into the muck and the other, still clad in the heavy overshoe, bore me up and gave me a lopsided gait.

We were spurred on by the sound of voices behind us. I could almost feel rifles aimed at my back but was afraid to turn around to see what was there. I fell headlong into the mire, as suction grabbed the big overshoe, and I lost my balance. I scrambled on hands and knees, sweaty and panting, until I found solid ground on which to stand upright. It seemed an eternity until we reached the other wood, where I had seen one of the parachutes go down. We made it without incident and no shots were fired.

We skirted the forest in a direction that took us away from the voices we had heard. After we had covered what seemed like a safe distance, I dove into the trees and began to remove my conspicuous clothing. There was underbrush there, so I was safe for awhile at least. I slipped out of my blue electric flying suit and was left with my wool O.D's and a sleeveless

Rescue 53

green sweater. After shucking the heavy overshoe, I thought I might be able to travel the lonelier roads unchallenged, notwithstanding having bare feet.

As the Luxembourg farmer led me across fields, through heavily wooded valleys and over steep hills, my mind was still too dazed to comprehend my situation. I felt very tired and my knee kept paining me, undoubtedly from the injury it had received from the parachute landing. What was happening seemed too simple and orderly. I had fully expected immediate capture or much suffering. The sun was so warm and the country so peaceful in its Spring beauty that the disturbance of war was unimaginable. The sight of Frasch's plane disintegrating in front of me and cartwheeling earthward kept playing and re-playing on the dark screen of my mind. Could I ever forget it? Why couldn't Jack have made it to the bomb bay and jumped with me? Was I being too lucky? It seemed too good to be true, like a scenario for a good book of fiction.

Finally the farmer stopped at a likely hiding spot for me. It was a small grove of what we would call Christmas trees at home. The forest floor was covered with a heavy mat of moss which would make an excellent bed. With gestures, my friend made me understand by pointing to his watch that I was to stay here until he returned for me at 6:00 p.m. My stomach was beginning to tell me how empty it was but I wanted a smoke more than food. I tried the word "cigarette" and, even with my American pronunciation, he understood perfectly, but shook his head to indicate he had none. He then turned and left me alone.

The prospect of sleep was welcome and I needed time to recover from the shock of all I'd been through, but again Jack crept into my thoughts. His loss would be a terrible blow to his wife, Edith and his son, little Jackie. It seemed only yesterday that Jack and his family had attended Christmas services with Jeanne and me in Lincoln, Nebraska. What would Jeanne's and my folks think when they learned that I was listed as "missing in action?" Our baby was due in a month or so and the shock to Jeanne might bring on a premature birth or worse. I forced myself to think more positive thoughts. Surely these people would get me back to England in a few weeks at most and then I could cable home.

As my confidence grew, I began to think I could pass myself off as a Luxembourg Partisan and I buried my dog tags, Class A pass, club memberships and anything else that would identify me as an American flyer. I patted down the soil and rearranged the moss. No one would ever find them. I certainly wasn't thinking clearly. I knew that, if apprehended with no identification, I could be shot as a spy. I couldn't even speak the language. But the act was done.

While I was preoccupied with my thoughts and burying my I.D., a thunder storm moved in and began pelting me with heavy rain. The trees didn't offer much protection, but I huddled under one of the small firs. My body was exhausted but my mind kept racing. For some strange reason I began sorting through events leading up to this last mission. Leo Carey was hard to understand. He was a Catholic and at first acted like he didn't have a serious thought in his head. But once we were in England, he began to change. He withdrew from the rest of us and each night paid a visit to the priest.

Jack, Bob and I had discussed our observation that Leo's religion wasn't making him happy. Instead he became more and more morose and fearful. He confided in me several times that God would bring us through safely but his words had a ring of desperation rather than conviction. He began to act like a man already sentenced to die and the rest of us began to feel that, if any of us were to be lost, Leo Carey would be that one.

Leo had also talked Lennon and Kerpan into going to church on Sunday, mainly because he thought somehow their involvement would add weight to his own desperate pleas for safety and that it was an absolute obligation to the crew as a whole. Even Jack, Bob and I were enough moved by his example to attend our own Protestant Easter Services. Sitting here in this young forest, I examined the possibility that perhaps Leo was right. It was highly possible that he had been saved, while Jack, who was on the other end of the scale from Leo's devout Christianity, was most probably lost.

Where did I fall in the scheme of things? Had God favored me in spite of my lack of devotion? He had certainly let me pass unscathed the very closest to death's door I could possibly imagine. Not only had the explosion waited until the very second I jumped, but also I had landed in tiny Luxembourg within calling distance of the German border. If I had jumped a minute earlier, I could now be in German hands, or certainly at least, be in Germany itself. Even Luxembourg had been described to us in briefings as predominantly of Nazi sympathy. Never in my life had a chain of events seemed more to be beyond mere coincidence. My immediate reaction was one of humbleness and a need to examine the possibility that I had drawn a little closer to the Creator. What was next in store for me?

The April shower had penetrated the thin canopy of branches over me, so sleep was now out of the question. To kill more time I began to take stock of the few valuables with me. There were a few English coins, three English pound notes, a silver crash bracelet given my by Jeanne's mother and my gold Phi Delt ring. The single article of food in my possession was a package of Life Savers. How odd that the most significant item in my possession should be called "Life Savers," I thought. I sucked one slowly, deliberating whether or not to ration myself, then ate them all with an abandon. The crash bracelet, in line with my previous reasoning, I decided to give away, for it identified me as a pilot and the English money should also go to these farming people. The ring, however, was my most prized possession, so I decided to keep it, at least for the time being.

Late in the afternoon I heard a rustling in the bushes, announcing the return of my new friend. We exchanged the whistle signals we had agreed on and he moved into view. He was accompanied by a middle aged man, short, sharp featured and wearing similar peasant garb. He seemed alert and intelligent and I assumed was probably the leader of this Partisan group. He took my hand and shook it with the same exaggerated enthusiasm as had the others. With a wide smile he said, "American, Comerade," emphasizing the last syllable of both words in French fashion. He identified himself as John Freres and my first friend as Robert Fairon.

He offered me a package of German Faro cigarettes which I eagerly accepted. He then produced from a sort of musette bag two quarts of wine and two huge ham sandwiches made with a dark bread. I gulped down one sandwich and drank as much of one bottle as I dared. The wine immediately produced a warm glow. I wanted a clear head, but they insisted I drink more and I finally emptied the bottle, fearing to abuse their hospitality unless I did so.

John then pulled from his bag an old shirt, pants, a ragged suit coat and a pair of light patent leather dancing shoes. It was apparent we were to travel to some distant hideout. While I donned the strange assortment of clothes, Robert was examining the bracelet and English money I had discarded, indicating that he would like to have them. With a sweeping gesture, I motioned that he was welcome to anything I had, little as it was.

About dusk we set out over the rain soaked fields and almost immediately were in heavily timbered mountains. Our path followed a deep ravine which split the hills in a winding course. I noticed that our leader took considerable pains to make use of cover and deduced it was meant to warn that there was always a chance of being observed from the opposite bank. "El Magne Cannon," he spat angrily as he pointed toward some concrete structures across the ravine. I understood him to say, by word and gesture that it was a German border defense line and was astounded to realize that I had parachuted barely a mile from it.

Shortly after leaving this military zone behind, we approched a spot where John indicated that one of my crew members had parachuted nearby. He let me know that I could call out for him. I called the name of each one, but the only response was a lonely echo. We began moving down steep slopes, through heavy underbrush and across several streams. I was soaked through and ached from head to toe. The dancing shoes, thin soled and loose fitting, often filled with dirt and gravel which I would have to stop and shake out. They were never intended for this kind of travel and offered little protection. Periodically I called out the names of my friends, but received no response.

As darkness fell, I was convinced it was hopeless to continue calling. We kept travelling in a southerly direction away from the German border, avoiding the main trails and roads. Many times we crossed wet plowed fields and walked through marshes to avoid being seen. For over a kilometer we fought our way through an almost impenetrable patch of Scotch Broom and I cursed many times at the branches that held me back. I was dead tired and now the dirt in my shoes had turned to mud which oozed between my toes at every step.

I was beginning to feel I couldn't take another step when we reached a main road and stopped to eat the lunch that was intended for the crew member we had been unable to contact. John, noticing my fatigue and visible limp, insisted that I drink the second bottle of wine. By the time I had finished it, I was half drunk and, when he indicated that we were half way to our destination, it scarcely registered. Distance meant nothing. My head was light and my eyes no longer focused. The sky had cleared and the stars were shining. In my condition they looked to me like comets.

Robert began talking and gesturing. Even in my befuddled state I understood that the road ran through a village where German soldiers were quartered. We were to walk at fifty pace intervals. He would lead and would be carrying a cigarette which he would use to signal us. If anyone approached, John and I were to dive into the ditch and lie face down. Following their example, I walked on the shoulder where our footsteps were muffled. I was instructed to watch behind me for anyone approaching.

A bicycle guard approached and we slid into the ditch. I hardly dared to breathe and my heart pounded so hard that I was sure it could be heard ten paces away. The danger passed and we straggled on. As we passed the German lodging place, a dog barked in alarm. I was certain it would bring someone to investigate but my friends informed me later with sly humor that the Germans were afraid to come out in the dark. I speculated that some of the Luxembourg Partisans may have given them good reason.

All went well. We continued on and, when we came to an open and less populated area, John became quite talkative. By selecting key words carefully, we were able to put skeleton sentences together to form a sort of universal language. I was to find out later that this was the medium by which nearly all of these men of many languages in the European underground melting pot could make themselves understood.

Many questions were asked about the plane I flew and the invasion which they expected to come soon. John told me he had just escaped from a German prison camp where he had endured seven months of hard labor. Bitterly he explained that the German tyranny over Luxembourg was the worst kind of oppression. The Germans were the only ones who were getting enough food or clothing.

Everyone was impatient for the invasion to begin, he told me. Shaking his fist, he vowed they would kill every German when the Allies arrived. To add weight to the promise, he produced a German Luger pistol, probably taken from some unfortunate German soldier, and I knew that he wasn't afraid to use it. This all came from a little middle aged man who was well beyond the boyish ideas of gangsterism, but had been filled with insane hatred by the atrocities of the Germans. For him this manner of life was beyond endurance. A man who ordinarily would be occupied with the peaceful pursuits of life, had now become a cold blooded murderer, like many Nazis themselves. I was secretly glad to have this man as a friend, rather than an enemy.

Eventually we left the main road and began climbing a hill so steep I thought I would never make it. My feet were leaden. It was an effort to pick one foot up and put it past the other. We were entering a little Luxembourg village and a half moon peeking between clouds cast enough light to make visible the church steeple. Closely clustered houses huddled around the church as if they counted on that holy place for their physical protection.

Not a gleam of light showed from behind black-out curtains and I guessed that it was well past midnight. I gathered from the talk exchanged between my two companions that this was our destination, and soon Robert left us behind to make arrangements in the village. When he returned a few minutes later, we crept stealthily along the worn cobblestone streets.

A house no more imposing than the rest and located in the heart of the village was the rendezvous point for the Partisans. Tiny cracks of light escaping through the edge of the window casings at this late hour hinted that this was no ordinary farming community. A network had been set up to thwart the Germans. Robert tapped a signal on the door and it opened almost immediately. A stranger led us to another door that opened into a lighted room, where I stood blinking as I waited for my eyes to adjust to the light. A farmer and his wife were the only persons present in the simple room. They eyed me curiously but looked somewhat frightened. I gathered their involvement with the movement had been trivial up until I stepped in the door. Now they were about to be a part of the resistance that could cost them their lives, if apprehended. Once they had recovered their composure they were roused into action. I certainly was not the picture of a daring young American airman. My torn and muddy, ill-fitting clothes, my almost bare feet, my scratched and bruised face, combined with shoulders sagging from exhaustion brought from them every hospitable urge.

The best chair in the house was drawn up near a fire on the hearth and the man went to get some dry clothes. The woman brought a pitcher of ersatz coffee, black and aromatic, along with hot milk which she poured into a large porcelain bowl. It held at least three cups, but this motherly woman wasn't satisfied until I had drunk three bowls of the mixture and downed four big slices of heavy dark bread spread with pure white butter and thick jam. I was so tired I could scarcely chew, but the attention was welcome.

The farmer, Joseph Fairon was of medium build, had a shock of curly black hair and a Charlie Chaplin mustache. His blue eyes, like Robert's, were rimmed with black lashes and he had a knack of adding an impish sparkle to them that belied his age. His wife was plump, giving a general impression of roundness, a plain round face with round brown eyes behind thick horn rimmed glasses. Her brown hair had probably never seen a hair dresser and looked unkempt. I learned that Joseph was Robert's brother and that he and his wife were both in their forties. I was puzzled that she would look so much older than he. Perhaps life under the Germans was harder for the women.

While I was eating, the other four talked in their French-German patois about what to do with me. Suddenly the door opened and a baby-faced boy of about sixteen stepped in. He joined the conversation and his elders stopped to listen to him as if he had something important to say. To me, Albert seemed a very ordinary, if somewhat overgrown boy, not quite man enough to shave. In America we would say he wasn't dry behind the ears. But in these war years, a Luxembourg lad nearing the age for conscription found it necessary to grow up hastily.

The two men who had brought me here checked the time and indicated that they had to return to their homes. I felt ashamed of my fatigue when I realized that for them their journey was only half over. We shook hands and I thanked them many times.

The Fairons
They hid me in their house after parachuting.

The Fairons

The two men left and Mrs. Fairon motioned for me to come with her. I followed her broad back up a narrow winding stairway from the kitchen. I was not allowed to use a light, but enough filtered in from the hallway that I could see an old four poster bed covered with a bright red quilt. The pillow was as wide as the bed and I discovered it was filled with something like nut shells to give it the appearance and feel of an oversized bean bag. A plain table and chair, along with the bed completely filled the forepart of the room. To the back were racks from the ceiling on which hung an assortment of ham, bacon and other cured meats. Not being refrigerated, the room smelled like a smokehouse and it was so overpowering I opened the window. Later I learned that it was to be closed during the day, a precautionary measure, as the German family living directly across the street were thought to be Nazis sympathizers.

Once my head hit that lumpy pillow, I thought I would immediately fall to sleep but the events of the day kept playing and replaying in my mind. The sight of Frasch's ship disintegrating before my eyes and diving earthward affected me more than the demise of our own ship, for I had seen practically nothing of the pyrotechnics surrounding us. The fire aboard ship had been out of my line of vision and I never saw the burning ship up close after it had crashed. In my numbed state I seemed incapable of comprehending the immensity of what had happened. Instead, between fitful sessions of sleep, where I seemed to find myself looking at that bright red ripcord handle and wondering if my parachute had opened, I would also see other parachutes drifting earthward all around me with giant hams swinging under them. I would awaken filled with nausea induced by the strong odor of the cured meats. I'd drop off again into that deathly silence I experienced while hanging in the snow cloud. How strange the way sleep weaves dream and reality together.

The next morning I awakened in my strange surroundings, not quite sure where I was. When Mrs. Fairon discovered that I could scarcely move, she hovered over me like a mother hen, bringing hot water for a soothing bath, followed by the regular simple European breakfast of coffee, bread and jam. Even the slightest activity left me exhausted and I was ready to sleep again. For two days I awakened only long enough to eat. At first Mrs. Fairon had seemed somewhat in awe of me, but now she treated me like a son, especially when I told her about Jeanne and the baby. After that she was as attentive as my own mother had been when I was stricken by some childhood illness.

Eventually my scratches healed, my bruises faded and my swollen knee began to return to normal. As vigor returned, so did my need to communicate. I learned that, not only did Mrs. Fairon prepare food for me and the two men, but also for an aged grandmother and a young child. The latter I never saw during my stay. In addition, her duties included milking and churning as well as all the other household chores. No wonder she looked older than her years.

The meals were the barometer of how these people were suffering under Nazi rule. All the meat the Fairons had came from my little room. It was a year's supply and Mr. Fairon explained that even this had to be kept from the Germans. All of the calves had to be sent to market where the Germans slaughtered them for their own use. Their greed left the farmers nothing for breeding purposes. Such a short-sighted policy inevitably brought about a dwindling supply.

Cows were expected to produce staggering quotas of milk, butter and cheese and the chickens an impossible number of eggs. There was nothing left then, but what little the farmer could withhold and hide away. As German military successes decreased under Allied pounding, the bolder the farmers became in reserving food for their own use. They ground corn and wheat by methods as primitive as those employed by Eighteenth Century American pioneers. Potatoes were the only staple of which they had plenty. They were filling and excess quantities were used to make up for the foods that were missing.

Shortages of other necessities were just as critical. During my stay here I was told that some city people had passed the long winter months by staying in bed all morning and retiring early in the afternoons. There wasn't enough fuel for fires nor enough food to heat their bodies. Civilians were allowed three cigarettes a day, imitation tobacco at that, and army men seven. Good wine, as necessary to most Europeans as coffee is to Americans, was doled out in a quart a month quantities. Few people here had a new suit of clothes or a new dress in the last four years and what Nazi clothing was available was made of a far from durable, thin wood fibre. Practically no one had tasted sugar, coffee or spices in this same length of time. There were no replacements for broken down machinery, worn out household equipment or miscellaneous hardware. And these were the rich in some ways, for they were farmers and had food and wood for fuel, whereas city people had nothing. The Nazis had taken it all.

My lunches and dinners consisted of a huge amount of potatoes, a small piece of fatty pork and cooked cabbage. Almost every day it was the same. I usually had extra bread and butter but the bread was black and of very coarse grain. I did get a bit of honey once and an ample supply of jam. Coffee was made of barley and oats. On my birthday, which came on the third day of my stay, Mrs. Fairon fried me a brook trout which her son Albert had caught especially for me, since he heard me telling that it was my birthday. Mr. Fairon even managed a couple of bottles of weak beer. He also secured from a little Partisan fellow named Pierre a pack of twelve cigarettes each day, a present which I accepted not knowing of their acute shortage. Later I came to believe that the men were depriving themselves of their own cigarette rations, just so I could smoke. I had never known such whole hearted and unparalleled generosity as I received here in Luxembourg.

When at last I could walk around, I began to explore my surroundings. I had needed the time for my natural good health to restore my body, but now I was curious. I began to hobble around and discovered that a small door in my room led to a hayloft on the back side of the house. It was on a level with the street. The house nestled into a hillside with the second story flush with the ground in the rear. It was here Mr. Fairon kept his harnesses, some small pieces of farm equipment and a huge supply of potatoes.

Square holes in the concrete floor allowed hay to be forked directly into the mangers below. I spent considerable time pacing back and forth, as I exercised my gimpy leg, and often looked down at the cows. They chewed their cuds contentedly and looked up at me with some curiosity. The idea of a barn attached directly to the house was amazing. The kitchen door opened right into the barn, where there were six cows and two or three dozen chickens, literally members of the household.

The barn was kept as neat and clean as the rest of the house. Straw on the floor was changed so often that the manure scarcely had time to cool. Mrs. Fairon used as much diligence cleaning the barn as she did emptying my chamber pot. The tile walkway was spotless and there was scarcely any odor, only the sweet smell of cows' breath as they munched contentedly.

They even had individual drinking fountains that came on when nuzzled.

When not pacing up and down the concrete floor and watching the cows peer up at me inquisitively through their feed chutes, I spent considerable time gazing at the surrounding countryside through cracks in the door to the street. From my vantage point I could see a large farmhouse across the street whose occupants, Mr. Fairon informed me with animated disgust, were unsympathetic toward the Allies. Beyond that house and the flat fields to the West lay the English Channel. For several days I eased the monotony and my resulting boredom by watching the outside activity through those cracks.

The sights I could see from my peepholes were my whole entertainment. I watched the farmer harness his plow horse and oxen. The women came out to gather eggs from the strawstack in front of the house. One of the girls was slim and attractive, reminding me that I was a young male and too long away from my wife.

Occasionally men in uniform came into view and I learned to tell the soldiers from the mailmen and the town police. In the evening children gathered to play a game in the street, something like "London Bridge." It was during these times that it was difficult to understand why certain men should be so perverted as to be willing to disturb such peace. I wondered if those happy children were aware of the tragedy that was being played out and what they would do if they knew a man from one of those airplanes which they "oh'd" and "ah'd" about, when our formations passed over, was barely fifty yards away.

I hoped my son or daughter would never be placed in the position these children were in but I felt a throat swelling pride when our Forts and Libs passed over. Somehow I felt their mere presence brought a message of hope to these people and strengthened their resolve to resist the forces that overwhelmed them. It was easy to back away from the knowledge that just a few days ago I was up there dropping death and destruction down on people just like these.

But our boys died, too. The little man they called Pierre, who had been a waiter in a Paris nightclub, relayed the information that a man's remains had been found with the wreckage of our plane. He said that there were three rings on the left hand and there was an officer's cap nearby. This just had to be Jack Farmer. Though I had thought all along that he hadn't made it, there was still some small part of me that clung to the hope that he had shared the miracle that saved me. Genuine grief welled up and I swallowed hard.

The days continued to drag by slowly. At first, thinking that my stay in Luxembourg would be short lived, I disregarded the possibility of a cigarette shortage and passed the weary hours consuming a whole pack of twelve each day. Later, when I realized that the supply was uncertain, I tried to ration them by taking a few drags, pinching the butt until it was extinguished, then relighting it later. Pierre promised me some books and Albert produced one of his grammar school geography books which was written in French. This wonderfully simple book proved to be a big help in understanding the language. Since I remembered something of my own grammar school days, I played a sort of word matching game, matching what I knew of the subject to the French words and actually "reading" the pictures. I spent many hours studying the area I was in, trying to learn possible routes of escape to Spain or Switzerland.

One evening Mr. Fairon, looking pleased, came to my room and motioned for me to come with him. Since I had only a fleeting impression of the house the first night I was there, it was with considerable pleasure that I found he was inviting me to join the family in the living room. This house which served as a safe haven for me, seemed to step back in time. The furniture was heavy and dark, made to last, not for beauty. A Grandfather's clock stood in the corner. The most modern piece in the room was a Singer sewing machine, vintage about 1920 or so. There was a stone sink in the kitchen, a ceiling height oak dish cabinet, a tremendous old wood stove and an assortment of utensils and dairy equipment hanging on the walls. In one corner was a cream separator and in the other a huge boiler for rendering fat and making soap.

In inviting me to their living room, I knew at once that the Fairons had sensed my boredom and were taking a serious chance to have me with them. It was a typical family scene, Mrs. Fairon peeling potatoes for the morrow, Albert reading the paper and Mrs. Fairon's old mother, whom I now met for the first time, knitting socks. Feeling that I was now a part of the family, I sat down opposite Mrs. Fairon, with the potato basket between us and began peeling potatoes. They laughed as though it were a good joke, for normally her husband would have the more important duty of reading the daily paper.

Mr. Fairon took the paper from Albert and showed me an item that boasted the military had shot down five hundred American bombers in eight days. Knowing that it was a Nazi controlled publication, I calculated that a more realistic figure would be about half that many planes, still a terrifying number. Occasionally we interrupted our potato peeling with what amounted to language lessons. We discovered that certain German words, because of their similarity to English, were easier for me to understand than French. I picked up such words as essen, goot, nein, varm, kalt and numerous others used in everyday conversation. We mimicked the sound of farm animals and pets and named them for each other, occasionally breaking out with spontaneous laughter.

A common housefly happened across the big table and I saw a mischievous twinkle come into Mr. Fairon's eyes. "Verstand flea?" he asked me, glancing at the table.

At first I thought he meant the fly, but then he hopped his finger along the back of his arm. "Verstand," I said proudly. "Anglaise, flea auch." I didn't know I was mixing my German and French, but he understood.

He then took off his old suit coat and pointed at it saying "Gestapo, Goebbels, Hitler," with a look of contempt on his face. Then he got on his hands and knees and drug his coat along the floor jerkily. His meaning was unmistakable that the Germans referred to were such lousy characters that their clothes could creep along by themselves. At the same time he scratched his back furiously and laughed heartily at his own joke. It was so well done that my laughter joined his for a long time. It struck me that his was an amazing display of defiance and said much about Joseph himself. These same people had spoken in whispers and considered every action aside from suspicious neighbors, but they were still undaunted.

As the days passed, Mrs. Fairon took even more pains to keep me happy. She always gave me the best cuts of pork and filled my plate with more food than I could eat. She emptied the pot for my toilet almost as soon as I had finished, a situation created by their recognizing that I couldn't use the outhouse without arousing suspicion. She fretted because my knee didn't recover as quickly as she thought it should. A day never passed but what she asked concernedly about Jeanne and the baby we were soon to have and, whenever any of her trusted friends paid her a visit, she would dash upstairs to ask me for the pictures of Jeanne which I carried, intending to show them to her guests. I know too that she was considerably impressed that Jeanne was an American wife wearing a WAAC uniform, especially a wife married to a flyer they harbored.

She may have just naturally been a motherly person, but I believe part of it could be attributed to the fact that her own son was nearing the age when he would be snatched up for the German army. Albert, however, had ideas of his own about a future military career. One day he took me into the hayloft where I had been getting my daily exercise and pulled down a sheaf of wheat, one of several I had noticed draped over the rafters. He carefully untied the bindings and proudly revealed a shiny, new 14 gauge, double barreled shotgun. Wiping each piece carefully, he patted it as if it were alive, then produced several shells. He and his father had removed the shot and replaced it with a solid pointed piece of lead. He grinned and pointed the assembled but unloaded gun at the sheaves of wheat, pulled the trigger and said, "American, Anglaise debarquer, Allemand ist caput!"

This baby-faced boy, still too young to shave and his father, in spite of the odds against them, were ready to do battle against the Germans. Their focus was on revenge. Nothing else mattered.

On the fifth night there was a great parley at the Fairon home. Pierre had brought several of his Partisan friends, a motley collection of determined men, to decide what should be done with me. Two of these were portly well dressed gentlemen, who carried an air of business importance, but they seemed to be there only for giving assent or dissent to the decisions of the others. There was a scholarly looking fellow, wearing horn rimmed glasses, who acted as spokesman. He spoke a little English and it turned out his primary purpose was to get my description to be used for a fake Belgium passport. Belgium was the place where most underground Partisan groups were hidden.

One of the men was a fat sloppily dressed individual who was a little drunk. He too could speak some English but professed a dislike of Americans, saying they liked only money, whiskey and women. In spite of his apparent dislike, he conveyed the information that two of the boys from my crew had been located and would be joining us here tonight. Happy as I was to hear this, I hadn't the slightest idea who to expect, but contented myself in hoping that one of them would be Jack, Leo, or Bob, my fellow officers.

Shortly after we had gathered in the living room, Mr. Fairon's brother, Robert and the little man John Freres, who had helped rescue me, walked in with two men whom I did not at first recognize. The two strangers had on old worn-out clothes many times too large for them and both wore battered caps slouched over their eyes. As they removed their caps and said my name, I recognized them to be none other than Bob Korth and Joe Kerpan.

Joe looked to be in great shape, but Bob's face was a ghastly white and I feared he had been injured, even suffered a mental breakdown. "What the hell is wrong with you, Bob?" I asked.

With a weak smile he replied, "I ate some damned pork that made me sick. I have just about turned myself inside out the last couple days."

It was such a relief to be together again and in relatively good shape that we did a lot of hand shaking and back slapping, as we laughed at the odd assortment of clothes we wore.

Bob told how he had delayed his jump from the burning ship, until he saw through the rudder pedal openings from his nose compartment below Jack and me, that we were ready to go. He had removed his earphones in preparation for the jump, so that explained why he hadn't heard me call him on the intercom. Then, when he saw my feet leave the rudder pedals, he had dropped through the nose wheel hatch and Leo was to follow right after him. Bob's jump must have been timed almost identically with mine, for the ship exploded immediately after he dropped through the hatch. He had been forced to delay pulling his ripcord until he was about a thousand feet above the ground, for the burning ship followed him down. When he pulled his ripcord, he hit the ground almost at once and the ship crashed only a short distance away. He lay there stunned, watching the Germans approach, but Partisans reached him first and fairly whisked him out from under the noses of the enemy.

Joe, who had an intense fear of water and once before had said that he would refuse to bail out over the Channel, ruefully told what happened to him. "With our ship on fire and all hell around us, all I wanted to do was get out of that mess. Damned if I didn't land square in the middle of the river between Luxembourg and Germany. I got out of my harness in record time, let me tell you. A couple of peasant women brandishing butcher knives came running toward me. I didn't have time to be afraid of the water. I got the hell out of there. After all I'd been through, I didn't want to get cut up by a couple of women."

He and Bob were reunited at a cave where four young Luxembourg men were hiding out to avoid German conscription. "Did they tell you Carey was killed?" Bob asked.

"Carey? I thought it was Jack," I answered.

"No, no, it was Carey. They found him next to the ship and he had a Holy Mary chain around his neck. He was hit by a piece of the wing when the ship blew up. They figure his parachute caught fire."

"My God! That's terrible. What a horrible way to die!" I had a vivid picture of him plummeting earthward, knowing that it was the end. It was hard to accept. "But look, Pierre told me it was the pilot. He said he had three rings on his left hand and there was an officer's cap nearby. Jack was the only one who wore a uniform that day and I know he was the only one who wore three rings."

"No," Bob insisted. "It was Leo. He wore a Holy Mary cross. I heard they buried him in Hipperdang."

"Could they both have been killed? I'm almost sure Jack didn't have a chance to get out; and yet you say the body had a Holy Mary Cross on it?"

John Freres evidently understood enough of our conversation to join us and say "Deux comrade caput. Hipperdang," and he held up two fingers so there would be no mistake. For a moment we stood in stunned silence. We hadn't been certain that we had lost even one of our crew and now this news was a blow we hadn't expected. I felt it in the pit of my stomach and it served to further my belief that some Divine providence had spared me.

The Partisans continued their meeting and our scholarly friend agreed to have passports for us in three or four days. Since Bob was sick, it was arranged for him to take my place and Joe and I would be taken to a nearby village. When he was well enough, Bob would join us and we would travel together to Belgium. From there, we were told, we would be taken by plane back to England. Other secret flights had been successful and it all sounded very good.

On the way to our new haven, Joe told me that Butler had been picked up by some Partisans and was already on his way to Brussels to take this same secret flight. One of the men produced a note in Butler's hand writing confirming the plan. Joe also told me that one of our men, one of the taller ones which could have been Standridge, Suber, or the new radio man, had suffered a blow to the head during his parachute landing. Shaken and in shock, he had run around in circles until another crew member who landed nearby corralled him. The delay had been costly, for both men were picked up by German patrols. The Partisans advised us that two others were also taken prisoners so, with two dead and us four who had escaped, the whole crew was accounted for.

In these times there wasn't much that could be said that would adequately show my appreciation to the Fairons, but I tried. The Kirsch residence where Joe and I were taken was a veritable paradise. We were given a bedroom which we guessed was either Mrs. Kirsch's personal boudoir or a lavish guest room. The bed and two huge clothes cabinets were of the very finest heavy carved oak. There were beautiful tapestries hanging on the walls and an intricate hand crocheted covering on the bed. Another item which I was to learn later adorns many of Europeans' finer beds, was a tremendous downy comforter, but I found it so warming that I'd toss it off during the night. These people were not peasant farmers. Everything in the home reflected the prosperity they enjoyed during peace time. Joe and I, in our rustic state, were even reluctant to use the chamber pots in the bathroom. Our hosts were so hospitable that we finally relaxed and sleep that night was right next to heaven.

In the morning we met Franz Kirsch, the oldest of four brothers. Husky and intelligent, he looked at us through heavy glasses. It was plain he was the business head of the household and principal host as well. The father, a German type sporting a large mustache and a huge pot belly, acted as manager, almost an honorary position, as we learned that Franz directed all of the farming operations.

Mrs. Kirsch, stooped and middle aged, wore a rather sad and put-upon expression. Like Mrs. Fairon, she too carried a heavy load, even in this prosperous household. There were two charming girls, a serious minded eighteen year old and a most flirtatious young woman in her early twenties. The household also included a very fashionable looking aunt who spoke some English. She seemed to have travelled widely and was not accustomed to putting her hands to farm work. It was easy to imagine a problem between her and the hard working Mrs. Kirsch.

After breakfast, Franz took us to his room where we were to remain out of sight during the day. Joe and I discovered a door that led into a haymow overlooking a large dairy housing about thirty cows. We were startled when the hay at the base of a big stack began to move and stood amazed as a blonde head poked through. A young man, grinning sheepishly, crawled out. He was followed by two others, all of army age. Evidently expecting us, he asked with a French accent, "American pilots?"

"Yes," I answered and then, searching for words in my scanty French vocabulary, I managed, "Vous cultivateur?"

"Non, non, non, Lutserbush soldat," he explained. In the same universal language that the Partisans had used, the boys began to piece together their stories.

Luxembourg boys were being conscripted into the German infantry, mostly for "cannon fodder," and these three had found themselves forced to fight on various fronts against men with whom they had no quarrel. One, a dark Italian looking lad, had fought in the Grecian and Russian campaigns and then was sent to fight the Yanks and Tommies in Italy. During the confusion of the Allied landings, he took the opportunity to escape and had been at the Kirsch's about a month.

The tall, blonde handsome fellow and the third member of the group, who resembled Robert Taylor, the American movie star, had both fought in the Russian campaign. On their first furlough they made their escape to the Kirsch's and had been living in their straw cave for the last nine months, scarcely daring to come out except for meals. They indicated that the Russians were fierce fighters and seemed like demons possessed.

None of the three could speak any English but the one who looked like Robert Taylor had read German movie magazines and had seen American films with French and German subtitles. As we became better acquainted, he took great delight in mimicking the stars. He put together a scene between Betty Grable and Clark Gable. "My darlink, I lauve you," he would say in a rather hilarious mixture of French and German accents or "Kiss me, my darlink." It was a bit of levity which lightened the seriousness of our situation and we had a good laugh.

The blonde fellow very seriously taught me to say,

"Vivigatit. Gie mein base" but didn't tell me what it meant. He indicated that I should say it to one of the Kirsch daughters to test my language ability. At the first opportunity, I rattled off the words to Anna, the serious one. She immediately flushed a bright crimson and rushed out of the room. It was only then that I knew I'd been had. The jokesters howled with laughter and then explained that I had said, "I love you. Give me kisses." I was relieved that it wasn't something that could have gotten me thrown out of the house.

The two girls had the job of serving the food their mother cooked and they also cleaned the house every day. Even so, they found time to visit with Joe, and me and our three new friends. The boys chatted familiarly with them and eventually I learned that the one who looked like Robert Taylor had wooed and won good natured Maria. I meditated that if there was anything serious to their love affair, Robert Taylor had better look after his interests, for Maria was casting many shy looks in Joe Kerpan's direction. In my estimation, serious Anna, with her red kinky hair, was less comely but had more personality than a dozen Marias. Her brown eyes were deep, thoughtful and intelligent and, although she rarely spoke, her eyes said much. She, like young Albert Fairon, was always consulted by members of the family in making household decisions in spite of her youthfulness. This was not surprising when one learned that she had spent six months in a German work camp for women. She had learned what suffering meant and she knew that silence was her greatest gift.

Mr. Kirsch enjoyed socializing with the three deserters, Joe and me, along with the two girls. He had Anna bring out the family album and he spent an entire afternoon telling us all about each and every picture. Here was a picture of his fifth son who was killed in battle. Here was one of Anna in her German uniform and with her German girl friends. Here was another of some close relative who had been shot by the

Gestapo or one who had not been heard from since he was taken to a German concentration camp. Mr. Kirsch told these things as naturally as if they were inevitable happenings among all Luxembourg families. I marvelled at his matter of fact tone and also at the fact that he was giving us shelter right under the Nazi's noses.

That evening Franz brought together a group of Partisans, I felt mainly to allow them to see what American flyers looked like. Somehow our presence amongst them had revived a courage that had laid nearly dormant since the beginning of the war. The crowded room overflowed with their boisterous talking and boasting of concealing Americans from the Germans and they seemed to forget all caution for suppressing the noise from anyone passing outside. They found it immensely gratifying that one of their number was concealing Americans from the oppressors. Though they were careful to conceal their curiosity of Joe and me, we caught them covertly scrutinizing us many times.

Our friends decided for us that we would leave for Belgium the next afternoon. Each was anxious to be the one to tell us that we would be back in England within eight days. Pierre gave us more cigarettes and presented me with a new cap, the sort farmers wore. Franz brought out suits and shoes for the two of us. There seemed to be no end to the favors bestowed on us by our new friends in this tiny country of Luxembourg.

"Father"

Around mid-afternoon of the next day, Bob arrived from the Fairons and in very much better condition than when we had seen him last. Franz had arranged with a friend of his, owner of a butcher shop in Clerf, to pick us up in an old Model A Ford, a veritable treasure in this country where there were extremely few autos and virtually no gasoline. After thanking our many Luxembourg friends for their kind hospitality and agreeing to exchange correspondence after the war, we sneaked out to the delivery truck and were on our way. We were overwhelmed with gratitude for all the help these good people had given us with practically no regard for their own safety or that of their families.

The butcher, a man of some thirty years, drove the old Ford as fast as it would go, careening around sharp curves and using both sides of the road as he maneuvered it through wooded hills. Bob and Joe were hidden in the back and I sat in front. The butcher showed me an American 45 calibre pistol which we were to use if necessary. In about an hour we approached the outskirts of what appeared to be a good sized town. Remembering my geography studies back at the Fairons, I judged it to be Clerf. Hanging from every building in the town were huge red flags with black swastikas in the center. Was our driver about to betray us? It was a disturbing thought which I quickly pushed aside. Our recent friends just had to be everything they seemed. It was near dusk and the butcher explained that there were no Germans in sight because they were afraid of the Partisans.

We drove up to an imposing building, possibly a German headquarters, with a huge red flag hanging over the door. Our driver jumped out and, without a word of explanation, disappeared down a driveway alongside the building. Again the disturbing possibility of betrayal entered my mind. It was all I could do to keep from yelling to Bob and Joe to run for safety. Reason took over and I knew that if this was indeed a trap, the Germans would be waiting for us and escape would be impossible. My fears were allayed when the driver came running back, jumped in the truck and began backing down the driveway. Some cohort closed a gate behind us and we were cut off from the street. Seeing my bewildered expression, he grinned as he rousted out Bob and Joe and motioned for us to follow him to a shop in the shadow of the Nazi building. It was his butcher shop and he and his Partisan friends were doing business right under the noses of the Germans.

We walked into what turned out to be an office adjoining the butcher shop and, waiting for us inside, was our driver's wife, a very good looking woman who spoke a little English. After welcoming us, she explained that this was the end of our journey and that we were to continue on from here by foot. Our host and hostess insisted that we have some schnapps before leaving, so we all raised glasses twice to each other's health and the success of the Allies. Directing my question to her, I asked, "Aren't you afraid to live in the very midst of so many Germans?"

"Oh, I have two small children. They keep me busy and I think also help give us the appearance of ordinary people. We know that someday the Americans and English will come and help us get back our country and our homes."

The butcher took us nearly a mile outside of Clerf and turned us over to two fellows waiting on bicycles. We were on the main highway to Belgium and one of the guides directed us to walk singly about fifty yards behind them in order to avoid suspicion. It was totally dark as we set out.

All seemed to be going well when the guides stopped to let us catch up with them. They told us that the only course available would take us across a viaduct with a guarded station on the other side. We were to bunch up and wait for a signal when it was safe to pass.

It was a tense moment. With hearts pounding we clustered close to the leader, not wanting to be left behind when the moment came. Luck was with us. A train came roaring into the station and while the guards' attention was diverted, we dashed across without detection.

A mile further on we came to a house where a farewell party was in full swing. A group of Luxembourg boys who had been conscripted by the German army would be joining our trek to the Belgium border. For some reason the Germans were drafting Luxembourg boys in wholesale lots, while the young men of Belgium had not yet been called up in such numbers. These young men would hide out in forests or on farms.

There were wines and cakes on the table and women were constantly bringing more food as the group made merry. They must have dug deep into their food supplies in order to give the boys a proper send off. There was a feeling of sadness and grim determination under the merriment but, when it came time to leave, no tears were shed. This no doubt was one of many such partings that had been held in the last four years. Wives and mothers smiled and wished them well, not knowing when they would see them again, but taking some comfort in the knowledge they were thwarting the Germans.

We walked for the better part of the night and halted only to pick up more men. The night was so black we had to link hands in order to stay together. Somehow our guides knew the way across fields and through forests where we would not be observed. At one point we again had to cross the same railroad we had crossed before. A watchman carrying a lantern came our way. We flattened ourselves along the side of a hill above the tracks and literally held our breaths, as he passed by within a stone's throw.

More guides joined us, some carrying rifles. They circled us like dogs guarding a flock of sheep. Now and then one would help a man with a heavy suitcase, lead us around or through a barbed wire fence, or round up someone who was lagging too far behind. I marveled at how well this pipeline to safety was set up but, at the same time, the necessity for such a venture made it a gut wrenching experience. All these young men in civilian clothes having to leave their families was a sad commentary.

When we came to the border, it didn't seem possible that we could make it across. There was a main highway and a well lit sentry post blocking our way but our guides obviously knew how to bypass the danger point and brought us around safely. In a short time we joined a Partisan group who were in the much more serious and dangerous business of smuggling arms and ammunition across the border to the various groups hiding in the forests. We Americans were asked to carry gunny sacks filled with various sabotage implements and explosives. It was plain that this was their regular traffic and we were just a sideline.

At early dawn we reached the railroad station at Martelange, a small border town. There, the Luxembourg boys left us. Our guide at this point was a cocky Frenchman who wore a beret jauntily on the side of his head. He bought tickets for Bostogne, a small town about ten kilometers away. Feeling exposed and vulnerable, we sat in the station lobby and passed the time looking at the Nazi posters on the walls. One depicted Europe as a walled fortress surrounded by flames (the Allies) with a handsome German soldier serving as protector. The other showed tall stately men and women of the working class walking hand in hand with bigger than life men in Nazi uniform who were also serving as protectors. Some indignant

Belgian had flung mud at both posters. I thought, with an inward chuckle, so much for German propaganda.

When our train arrived, it turned out to be a single diesel driven car, like an American street car but running on the main line. We boarded the car with a group of working class people who paid no attention to us, though we felt our identity was patently obvious and we would be exposed at any second. We paused at a station and two ranking Nazi officials boarded and stood on a platform at the rear, very close to where we were sitting. We tried to be as inconspicuous as possible. It seemed my skin literally crawled, my palms began to sweat and I hoped there was no visible manifestation of my inner turmoil.

My feeling of alarm was somewhat alleviated when I saw a Belgian workman who was standing next to one of the Nazis deliberately hold his lighted cigarette against the man's uniform until it began to burn. When the stench of burning wool reached the officer's nostrils, he angrily began beating the spot with his hand. The workman nodded his head in a humble manner and said, "Pardon, Monsieur." The audacity of the act once again strengthened my feeling that the indomitable spirit of these people would carry them through whatever lay ahead.

One of the Nazi officers began talking with our guide. We were afraid that certainly we would be exposed, but he remained cool and talked casually with the officer and later even winked over the man's shoulder to reassure us. When we got off at Bostogne, he laughingly explained that actually he had initiated the conversation with the Nazi in order to divert his attention from us. He then went on to say that the other uniformed man was impersonating a Nazi policeman who would have made a pretense of arresting us, if we had been apprehended by the military. We would later then have been released. This was certainly a well thought out and efficiently functioning part of the underground.

From the station we were taken to an unpretentious looking beer hall where our guide awakened the family who lived in the rear of the establishment. A woman and her two very attractive daughters operated the place and welcomed us with a round of beers. The girls waited on us in such a matter of fact way, it was plain that they were familiar with this part of the Partisan effort. The younger girl showed us a picture of a young Canadian flyer who had written on the back of the photo, "To the loveliest girl in the world, Dave." He had stayed with them ten days before escaping to England. It was easy to see why he had fallen in love with her. She had a figure that would put Venus de Milo to shame and she was well aware of her charms.

Her sister, a sensible down to business type, took care of the details. The studious character back in Luxembourg had failed to deliver my promised passport, so it was necessary to get one here. She took Bob and me to a photographer in midtown Bostogne, an experience I would not soon forget.

We boldly walked out of the tavern with her between us. We hadn't much more than got out the door when a large formation of Belgian boys came goose stepping down the street. The girl explained they were being trained for work camps. They were dressed in black uniforms with red swastika arm bands and were singing a German marching song, but it was certain their hearts weren't in it. Some of them, no more than ten years old, their faces looked like rigid masks. There was no boyish exuberance here. It was a forlorn exhibition. As we walked down the main street, we came upon a group of these young boys standing idly in front of a confectionery store. A Nazi officer passed by and the boys, clicking their heels together sharply, piped in their young voices, "Heil Hitler!"

We only saw all of this out of the corner of our eyes, for we dared not pause to stare. This was the sort of thing we had seen in propaganda films back home. I had taken it all with a grain of salt, but now this was graphic confirmation of how far the

"Father"

Hitlerization of Europe had gone. My consternation and revulsion were almost overpowering.

The photographer who took our pictures was a Partisan. Once he had snapped Bob and me, he took another one of us with our arms around the girl. Later in the day the younger girl showed up with Joe and wanted her picture taken with all three of us. It occurred to me that she must have a whole rogue's gallery of sweetheart pictures to show to the next Americans or British who came along.

A Catholic priest who spoke excellent English came by the tavern. He wanted all the pertinent data necessary for radioing to England. In that way our families could then be notified of our safety. It seemed rather incongruous that this man of God should come to this unlikely place, but the war made strange bed-fellows.

Another English speaking fellow, a businessman from Bostogne, came to talk to us. He looked as though he belonged in the military, strong featured with steel grey hair and eyes to match. With much vigor and indignation he related stories of the atrocities the Belgians had suffered. He was in banking and real estate and felt so strongly about what was happening that he was more than willing to do all he could for the Partisan effort, while still maintaining his business front. When he told how the Germans were taking church bells to melt down for implements of war, he could no longer contain himself. Tears came to his eyes and his big frame began to shake with sobs. Embarrassed at his show of emotion, he hurriedly took his leave, saying venomously, "Those dirty bastards!"

The matron of the tavern was a fat little lady, with a heart as big as she was round. She took good care of us during our short stay and even cooked us a meal from her scarce city rations. While we ate, she showed us pictures of her four sons, three of whom were killed and one imprisoned by the Germans. The one in prison had found a Nazi officer molesting his sister. He had thrown a glass of beer in his face and knocked him down. He had been hauled off to prison without a trial.

A third daughter was married to John, an amiable French-Belgian who made an appearance at the tavern that evening, along with a couple of his Partisan friends. He carried a little English language book with him and was delighted to show off how much he knew. His attempt at conversation was interminable—long on time but short in content. There were long pauses while he hunted up each word, so long in fact, he would forget the first part of a sentence or even the thought he wished to convey.

They brought us some light overcoats, shabby but welcome, as the weather had turned cold. Since we were leaving as soon as it was dark, we knew we would need the extra protection. The pictures from the photographer had arrived and everyone worked at putting together the fake passports. The youngest daughter chose our new names. Joe was Martin Roger, Bob was John Guilliam and I was dubbed Renee George. As she tossed off the names, there was much laughter among her family and we learned they were names of former sweethearts.

When at last it was time to leave, wine was poured and toasts were made. The mother began to weep, sobbing loudly and shedding copious tears. Since the loss of her sons, she fancied every young man who came to the door a surrogate son. I tried to comfort her but she only wept louder, so the girls hurried me out behind the others. John, moved by the emotional fervor, could not contain himself and grabbed each of us in turn, giving us kisses on each cheek in true French fashion. It was the first time any of us had ever been kissed by a man, but we refrained from making any frivolous remarks.

When John's friends had led us to the outskirts of town, they told us that the priest had asked that we be brought to his home. There we would wait for arrangements to be made to fly us back to England. He didn't want any of the tavern people to know of his plans. Tavern keepers, regardless of their good intentions, had too much opportunity to let a careless remark reveal our whereabouts. The priest was waiting for us at his house a few kilometers outside Bostogne. A huge old place across the street from the church, it was where he lived alone, with only a part time housekeeper to interrupt his solitude.

We were shown to rooms on the second floor where we found comfortable furnishings and clean linen on the beds. Joe bunked alone, while Bob and I shared a room. Father, as we now addressed him, had spent the day preparing for us and had even rigged a blue light to lessen the chance that a glimmer might escape around the blackout curtains. He showed us the bathroom which held a homemade flush toilet, the first we had seen here or in Luxembourg.

We welcomed the opportunity to wash up and joined the Father refreshed. He offered us comfortable easy chairs and indulged us with good cigars and schnapps. This handsome middle-aged priest had made every effort to make us welcome. I think, while he undoubtedly led a lonely existence, he felt he was doing something to further the Resistance. We sensed that he was a leader of the Partisans and harboring escapees was something to his personal credit.

For the next five evenings we gathered in the pleasant room for a few "drops," as Father called his schnapps, and listened to "This is London Calling." There was a lot of speculation about the truthfulness of what we heard on the radio. At eleven P.M. sharp he shooed us off to bed, as if we were growing boys, then prepared his message for the morning service.

We had the run of the house. The windows were curtained and anyone who wished to see Father went to the church. There were plenty of English books in his library, so the time didn't drag. We were never hungry, as there was always bread and jam or honey and sausages and fruit. If the supply ran low,

Father merely called upon the members of his parish, saying that he wanted food for a needy family. His pleas were always generously met.

Father took his meals at a neighbor's and arranged for them to bring our meal in a bucket after dark. We eagerly looked forward to this meal, as it was prepared with as much care and skill as anything we had eaten in American hotels. There was always soup, followed by well cooked meats, a salad with sliced boiled eggs and real salad oil and always some excellent vegetables. It was invariably topped off with a pudding of some sort and we had plenty of wine or beer. After experiencing the meager Luxembourg fare, the food actually seemed lavish and we ate with considerable gusto.

The young mademoiselle who brought the food also cleaned our rooms, all on her own time and without being paid. As soon as we finished eating, she began washing the dishes and then did whatever cleaning needed to be done about the house. We began to feel a little guilty about accepting all this largesse, so we decided to take over mademoiselle's duties. One evening when she arrived, we were waiting to greet her with the little French sentences Father taught us, "Nous avons fait nos lits. Nous avons lave les vaiselles. Nous avons coupe du bois."

Mademoiselle was almost overcome with surprise and we were pleased that she understood us. In spite of our efforts to help, she continued to find things to do for us. Like the people in Luxembourg, the Belgians considered it their duty and actually a privilege to bend all effort toward thwarting the Germans.

One evening, Father related some of his wartime experiences. He was teaching language at a Catholic university near Marseille when the Germans came. The priest's home, best in the sector, was taken over by the Germans to be used as officers' quarters and the priests were stripped of all their personal belongings. He lost his auto, an expensive radio and all of his furniture and his room was occupied by a German colonel. The priests had just purchased for their own use a large barrel of very good champagne. The colonel hadn't noticed it in Father's room, so Father and the others contrived to carry it away a little at a time in open jars. At first the plan succeeded, but inevitably the guards posted around the house smelled what was being transported past their very noses. The colonel himself discovered what the numerous trips were all about and appropriated the rest of the champagne for himself and fellow officers.

The priests were allowed to take other rooms on the campus, so Father became well acquainted with the colonel who had taken his room. The colonel evidently had some small remnant of conscience, for he began apologizing for the inconvenience he had caused. He even gave back what was left of the champagne. About the time the U.S. entered the war, he paid Father a visit and made a very strange request. He said he knew when Germany had turned against Russia and the United States that the war was lost and he begged Father to hide him in this house until the war was over. Of course his answer was a resounding "No!"

Father's hobby was radio and anything having to do with electricity, and there were many examples of his handiwork around the house. His room was littered with tools and hundreds of small electrical parts. The radio in the living room, the special lighting arrangements throughout the house and the electric toaster were all the result of his fascination with all things electrical. He retrieved some of the valuable radio equipment from a Fortress and a Lancaster that had crashed near the parish and buried it in the back yard. He also had other secret hiding places for various pieces of electrical equipment, not willing to have them appropriated by the Germans.

As the days passed and trust grew, he showed us where he had buried hundreds of rounds of ammunition in the garden. This further confirmed our belief that he was the leader of the Partisans in that district, that and the fact that messengers regularly reported to him. He was not in the least afraid of the Germans. "They have come on inspection rounds quite regularly," he said. "On one such visit I demanded to know why they were bothering a poor parish priest." Chuckling at the memory, he went on, "They looked bewildered that I should question them, apologized and left without making a search."

"It seems," he explained, "that they are so used to people being intimidated by their mere presence that, when someone stands up and speaks boldly to them, they are somewhat nonplussed." The longer we knew Father, the more we respected him. The term "Father" had more than a clerical connotation to the parishioners whom he guided, served and protected.

We had continued to harbor not only the hope but the sincere belief that we would be back in England in short order, but there came a day when one of our Partisan friends arrived with the news that put an end to our optimism. We had never been briefed on methods of escape from the continent, but we knew that some of our fliers had made it. It was generally conceded that Spain or Portugal offered the best chance. We knew too that Switzerland presented a possibility, but there was an equal chance that we would be detained by the Swiss. We even toyed with the idea that a plane might land at some secret field in Belgium or France and pick up fliers who had parachuted over Europe.

It was a shattering blow when Father called us together and relayed the information that the Germans had discovered the secret landing field and, unless another one could be found, that avenue was no longer open to us. The messenger

"Father"

also brought the news that the Gestapo had broken up the underground chain and it was virtually impossible to get across the heavily guarded Spanish frontier. Everyone we had encountered believed that the Allied invasion of Europe was imminent and that the war would soon be over. The Fairons had even asked me to stay with them until it was over.

Father was also disturbed by the news brought by the messenger and sat in thoughtful silence for awhile. Finally he said, "I think the best plan is to send you to the Army Blanche. They surely will know what best can be done with you."

Neither Bob, Joe nor I approved of the plan. We knew precious little about infantry weapons and didn't relish the idea of fighting out of uniform. We were highly trained fliers and the thought of fighting on the ground with the Belgians and the French had no appeal for us, but there seemed no alternative. Although it went against every instinct, we finally agreed to go along with the plan.

In a couple of days a guide came for us and, after giving Father many hearty thanks, we were on our way. I walked about a hundred yards behind the guide while Bob and Joe were about the same distance behind me. We kept to the fields and forests, and the trip proceeded without incident. The guide motioned me to him at one point and in broken English began telling me about the activities of the Partisans living in the woods. He explained that the villagers provided most of the food and they made up the deficit by raiding the Nazis. Sabotaging was at a standstill just now, however, as they were awaiting word from the English and Americans about the invasion. He told me there was another American flier in the camp and I speculated that it might be Butler, our gunner.

This was going to be an interesting experience, to put it mildly, and I knew that we were going to have to dig deep and find inner resources to see us through the present uncertainties. When it seemed we would be back at our base in a matter of days, we felt that we could handle anything that came our way but now we would be fighting for our very survival.

We finally reached the Black Forest where the organization was bivouacked and were met by two guards at an outpost who took us the rest of the way. As we approached the camp we saw two men with wads of paper heading for the bushes to relieve themselves. One of them yelled a greeting in French. When we answered in English, he pointed excitedly to a third man already squatting on the forest floor. "American!" he shouted.

"Are you the American flier?" I asked the man in the embarrassing position.

"Yep," he answered matter of factly, "that's me."

Such was my introduction to Clarence Wieseckel, who I soon learned was called "Johnny" by the men in camp. Through much read American movie magazines, they were familiar with the pop song, "Oh Johnny How You Can Love" and thought the name was much better than the unfamiliar Clarence.

When he had completed Mother Nature's call and did the best he could with his makeshift toilet paper, we exchanged greetings in a more conventional way, then joined the Partisans in camp.

The Army Blanche

Our impression of the whole setup was most disappointing, as the Partisans were just finishing their evening meal. What a rag tag bunch they were. They looked more like hoboes than soldiers. Dirty and loud mouthed, the sounds of their bickerings filled the air and suggested there was no regard for leadership or order. There were about thirty of these young men and the thought flashed in my mind that surely one of them could have taken it on himself to dig a latrine.

Sitting down to a meal of potatoes and poorly cooked pork, we choked the food down, as fatigue washed over us. A sloppy individual somewhat older than the others swaggered up to us. His hair hadn't been cut for months. He wore a baggy old sweater, khaki riding pants and scuffed unshined boots, certainly not military attire, but we assumed he was the leader. I searched my mind for a suitable title but none seemed to fit. When he learned we were fliers, he offered us cigars, probably appropriated on a raid, but welcome nevertheless.

Johnny joined us and we exchanged information under better circumstances than the incident in the woods. He was a tall, sandy-haired, handsome man with a habit of cocking his head to one side in a sort of quizzical shyness. I took an immediate liking to this man who looked as if ministerial garb would have been more fitting than the American uniform he still wore. He had parachuted from his crippled Fortress and had traveled through the enemy's homeland for seven days and nights, sustained only by the rations in his escape kit.

During that time, he confided to us he had been seen and curiously eyed by many Reichlanders, but no one made any effort to detain him. He had been in camp about a week.

That night we slept on straw in a lean-to. It was bitter cold and there was only one blanket for the three of us new arrivals. We were packed so tightly in a row of bunks built for two that there wasn't room to turn over and the smell of unwashed bodies was overwhelming in such an undersized shelter. Sleep was impossible for us but those who were used to it snored, coughed, mumbled and cursed the night away.

With considerable relief I welcomed the dawn. I brushed the straw from my clothes, tried to stretch the stiffness from my aching back and picked my way through the rows of sleeping men. Except for their snores, the camp was quiet. I needed to examine the situation I found myself in and decide whether to make the best of it or plan to escape on my own. Considerable time had elapsed since the crash and I was growing more and more concerned about Jeanne. If Edith should get word that Jack was killed, she would undoubtedly call Jeanne and then Jeanne would fear I had suffered the same fate.

All sorts of disjointed thoughts came tumbling through my mind, as I wandered down a much-used trail. When a strange figure suddenly approached, I assumed he was on watch duty, but he looked more like a character out of a comic opera. He was a tall scarecrow of a man with an almost effeminate face topped by long bushy hair. He wore riding breeches and boots and had a long cape draped over his shoulders. He peered at me through horn rimmed glasses which gave him the owlish look of the proverbial absent minded professor.

As we passed on the trail, he nodded without so much as a grunt of greeting and continued his slow pace toward camp, his shoulders stooped as though the welfare of the place was his responsibility entirely. I saw him several times during the day, still with the same thoughtful bearing.

The Army Blanche

The day passed and there were many conversations with first one and then another of the men who wanted to know about our missions over Europe and the progress of the war. It made me realize how little we really knew. We just did what we were trained to do and had no more idea when or if the invasion would take place than did this motley group.

Johnny had been out on a raid with a group the night before. They were after Nazi building materials to expand the camp. Another lean-to was being built and they were putting the finishing touches on a vicious looking barbed wire lid that covered a four foot square hole in the ground. It was about four feet deep and I couldn't imagine what it would be used for. The cage like lid was supported at each corner by log corner posts. One of the men explained that the pit was to be used for prisoners. When he said that one of their group had stolen for himself loot that had been taken on a raid, I rather doubted that such harsh treatment would be used on one of their own, but didn't question it.

The food for the day was mostly potatoes, bruised and poorly prepared. It certainly didn't do anything to lift our spirits and I thought longingly of the good fare we had enjoyed at the priest's home. Bob, Joe and I spent the day chopping wood, taking out some of our frustration with each swing of the axe.

Along about five o'clock, one of the guards came crashig through the underbrush, winded by the exertion and flushed with excitement. When he met with the camp leaders, voices were raised and there was much gesturing. Theo, a red headed fellow I had become acquainted with, relayed the information that the Germans were coming. He had learned a little English during his high school days, enough so we could communicate.

In broken English Theo told how the fellow with the cape had fancied himself a martyr. On his own initiative he had entered the house of someone suspected of being a Nazi sympathizer and demanded eggs, threatening the household with a pistol. "Gif me ekks or I shoot," said Theo as he dramatized what the cape wearer had done.

Actually the victim of the raid was a Belgian in sympathy with the Partisans. Infuriated by what had happened, he called the police, giving them information about the location of the camp. If he was going to be robbed, he preferred the deed to be done by the Nazis alone, not by both the Nazis and the Partisans. The police had organized a posse of two hundred German soldiers and would arrive in a couple of hours.

There was some confusion among the men as they argued about the best plan of action. Some of the self styled gangsters wanted to get out their poor assortment of arms and offer some resistance. They had confided in Joe Kerpan, the Chicagoan, that they were really Chicago gangsters themselves, and perhaps some of them were. All they had was a machine gun with no tripod, taken from an English Lancaster, some double and single barrel shotguns, one or two rifles and a few miscellaneous handguns, scarcely any two taking the same ammunition and little available anyway. The idea of resistance died a quick death, as the wave of mob fervor subsided. Clearer heads prevailed and they decided the practical thing to do was to have a quick snack and retreat.

We had been here less than twenty four hours and alreay we were caught up in this cat and mouse game requiring constant vigilance, a game where the rules were as changeable as the weather and the hunter became the hunted and vice versa. Our hosts had been playing it for more than four years.

Strangely enough, the excitement gave us new respect for this unlikely crew who were doing all they could with practically no equipment, no organized support and no regular supplies. Now, with this threat of danger, we were sharing the same risks. We began to look at them from a different perspective. Their reaction to the crisis quickly revealed the characters of the men. Some began to laugh and joke to relieve the tension, others began whittling on tree branches, fashioning walking sticks preparing for a long march to another refuge. The boys were accustomed to this life and knew how to make the best of it. When necessity warranted it, their maturity surfaced.

The procession bordered on the comical with overtones of tragedy. A small two wheeled cart was piled high with corrugated metal for building a stove, all the large kitchen ware and various types of luggage. Each of us shouldered one or two gunny sacks of dishes, small equipment, food and whatever else was portable and deemed necessary. Some had bicycles and piled the rear carriers high with blankets, assorted clothing and personal belongings, while others carried nothing but their shotgun or rifle. A new chief, who had arrived to oversee the move, carried an outdated English Tommy gun.

With only the sound of our feet on the packed earth of the trail and the rattle of equipment to break the silence, we walked for a kilometer or so until we came to a main highway. Our advanced guards motioned us to move in bunches across the open area as quickly as possible. Occasionally we would stop to give the man pushing the heavy cart a chance to rest. During these stops, Theo and I and Freddie, another fellow I came to know, would carry on whispered conversations. Both of them were good looking Luxembourgers, especially Freddie who had a strong square face, brown eyes and a mop of curly hair. They insisted I share their cigarettes, though I could see they had only a few. They were pleased when I gave them some of the small supply Father had given me.

Theo had been a clerk or junior accountant in a business house before the war. Freddie had worked on a farm but had known Theo in school. He laughed when he told me about

Theo's beautiful sister and outlined her seductive curves with the motion of his hands. They both agreed it would be worthwhile to come to America, when I told them about my own three curvaceous sisters. Freddie was especially interested when I told him the blonde one looked like Betty Grable. I think every male in Europe had seen pin-ups of the luscious Betty.

Six or seven kilometers were behind us by the time it was dark. The leader halted us at a predesignated spot and in the dusky light we saw a long hay or straw shed that bordered a summer pasture surrounded by woods. It was dark inside the shed, but it didn't take us long to discover that the straw-covered floor was generously splattered with manure. The warm shelter was preferable to the cold outside, however, so we kicked aside what we could and arranged the straw to be as clean as possible. The night was even more miserable than the previous one, for we had to share our too few blankets with another contingent of men who had arrived from somewhere.

When I awoke, unrested from my fitful sleep, I discovered that some of the men had already left. They had picked a campsite across the pasture in the dense wood. The oldest man in camp, a forty-five-year-old red head with a grizzled beard, was construction boss and already had his gang putting up sleeping quarters, using the corrugated metal for the sides. I had no idea where the rest of the material came from, but it was obvious that these men had gone through this routine many times. When it was finished they had put together ten bunks, five upper and five lower, each wide enough to sleep four men. The cook and his assistant had their own quarters on the end of the building and they kept the supplies there under lock and key. Everything was camouflaged from the air and no trails were allowed to and from the camp. This time a long pit was dug to serve as a latrine and by noon we had a camp that would have pleased the toughest army sergeant. This day had taught me a lesson. It isn't wise to pass judgement on the basis of first impression.

Days passed with nothing to do but keep the camp going, loll in the sun and listen to the tales of those who had been on raids. The food had taken a turn for the better. Some of the men had appropriated a whole beef from a Nazi farmer's herd and on another raid they stole eighty kilos of butter from a creamery serving German soldiers. Some of the men on this raid were caught before they could get away and one had been shot at. In his desperate race to escape, he lost a shoe and had to walk thirty kilometers with only one. His price for freedom was one bruised and cut foot, while the others were taken with their loot to the local police station. When the sympathetic police heard their story, they gave them back the butter and let them go.

Our numbers had increased to the point where the limited shelter could no longer serve. We had been joined by two Russian escapees, a Belgian and several more men from Luxembourg. The camp chief who, because of his even nature and cool decisiveness, had earned my respect, now decided to divide up the group and establish another camp close by. He suggested that Bob and I go along with the contingent to help with the project, and I was delighted with the opportunity for some construction activity. The two Russians were going along and it would give me an opportunity to know them. They had been casting glances our way since they learned we were Americans.

We learned that they had been captured by the Germans at Stalingrad and taken to a prison in central Germany. They managed to escape and had walked some five hundred kilometers to Belgium. They had practically no food and were still wearing the tattered clothes they had stolen from some poor German peasant. One was on the short side, slight of build and beginning to bald. He was tanned from all the exposure, and I judged him to be in his late thirties or early forties. He told us he was married and had two children. The other fellow was about the same but rather nondescript and was content to follow the lead of his companion. They were not talkative and spent most of their time whittling on walking sticks. The first man was most handy with a knife and turned out a well crafted stick in no time at all.

As we trudged along toward the new campsite, they began to open up. We kept away from war talk for the most part, but we seemed to have a mutual high regard for each country's military accomplishments. They certainly weren't like the communist trouble makers we had once seen in the States. They were cheerful, easy-going men, possessed of inner drive and a certain fearlessness. It was easy to see that the Jerries would have difficulty defeating a nation of men like these.

The camp leader was such a man. I thought he was probably a French national. He never talked about himself but we could guess a lot. He had a steady unflinching gaze and was always calm. I never heard him raise his voice, though I sensed he could handle himself, should the occasion arise.

Before we reached our campsite, we came upon an old deserted chateau. We learned it had been the country estate of King Leopold's family. The grounds were quite well preserved and swept in wide terraces down to a beautiful little lake. The huge old structure, even in its state of disrepair, still seemed quite grand and it was easy to imagine that it had been the scene of many gala royal parties. Huge oaks guarded the entrance. A sign bore these words: "Arrete de Entre."

The inside, damp and smelling of decaying wood, still held evidences of former grandeur. The woodwork was intricately carved and there were many stained glass windows now missing pieces here and there. The hallways were laid with brightly colored tiles and once beautiful wall paper hung in shreds from the walls. At the foot of the winding tower staircase, we discovered hand painted canvasses of castle scenes and one of a coat of arms. Under other circumstances,

I would have given a lot to take them home as souvenirs.

Our footsteps were loud on the base floors and we could hear the squeaks and rustlings of resident rodents. I wanted to spend more time exploring the place, but we were here to scavenge what we could for building the new camp. It seemed almost sacrilegious to inflict more insult on this once proud example of royal living. The two Russians were in their glory as they worked like mad men, tearing up boards and saving every little thing that might be used in camp. The screech of nails being wrenched through old wood seemed like the cries of a wounded human. I left the place later that afternoon feeling as though I had seen the end of an era.

By the end of the next day the new camp was completed and, to my disappointment, Theo, Freddie and the two Russians were lodged there, while we Americans remained at the old site. The camp chief elected to command the new camp and left Renee, the cook, in charge of ours. I missed my friends, but Theo and Freddie often returned to sit by the campfire at night. Freddie told us the Russians were still working like crazy and seemed as happy as a couple of kids. Freddie rolled cigarettes for me. I simply could not learn how to roll one of the things. The tobacco always fell out one end or the other or they turned out to be camels (hump backed). We would sit and smoke as we talked and the war seemed far removed.

Even with the shifting of part of the camp population, we were still crowded for sleeping space. Bob, Joe and I had shared a four space bunk and now a tall lanky Luxembourger took the fourth space. Coupled with the fact that his size commandeered more room, his putrid breath and equally foul body odor were overpowering. We were so nauseated and revolted by him that there was much jockeying and outright trickery practiced, as we each wanted to get the spot the farthest away from him. We worked out signals for simultaneously turning over, so we always faced in the same direction as he did and wouldn't have him breathing in our faces. He was a fitful sleeper and we had to have a firm grip on the flimsy blanket or one or more of us would be exposed to the cold. It might have been funny if we hadn't been so uncomfortable. I even imagined I was beginning to smell like him. Soap and water weren't too plentiful but we did the best we could.

Renee took over his new position of leadership with great seriousness and soon proved he was as capable as any old hand. He was a short stocky fellow with pale blue eyes, a large nose and a small mouth better suited to a female face. His hair, thin and receding, ended in little ringlets in the back. He had been a barber in Luxembourg and, with his rather effeminate look, one might have expected him to be an object of ridicule but he was feared and respected by even the big men in camp. The cooking chores were handled smoothly by his assistant, so Renee busied himself with more administrative duties.

Actually he was a genius in the kitchen, making use of whatever was at hand. When one of the boys picked up a bottle of salad oil on a raid, Renee took several men to the cow pasture. Getting down on his hands and knees, he showed us how to cut a dandelion to get the tenderest leaves for a salad. Europeans have recognized and used the dandelion as food for many years, but probably most Americans view the lowly weed as nothing but a nuisance in their lawns. Renee's salad of chopped onions, dandelions and salad oil was as tasty as any I had ever eaten.

This many-sided character was gifted with a beautiful tenor voice. He had fought with German troops in an Italy based unit and had learned several love ballads as well as humorous ditties. Around the campfire at night he favored us with his songs. Our gang of rough necks was moved by the beauty of the ballads and sat completely silent, each with his own thoughts of love, home and family. One of the ditties I thought so funny, I copied down the words to take back to America.

> Der Spitzli, Der Spetzli
>
> Es sar schlugen sish swie Italiano
> Da gop es tsu lucken und su vinio
> Der ina der sproch ferracha du Lumpio
> Der undera der hout ine in de clumpio
> Sakrary Tomati saladuchi
> Imu festu auf de Dooly Duchi
> Und altz see nun varen halt caporio
> Da martin si vido Frisidio
>
> Auf inem boimly da sar un Spetzli
> Da spetzli das vetst Zich das Schwenzli
> Da commen swei bose Bubli Uchi
> Die voffen das Shpetzli mit Steinli
> Unt alz zinum troffen sein Schwenzli
> Da marte das Shpetzli ein Tensli
> Fun der Schpitzli du Spoimli Om Shtemli vor bie
> Is unten argekommen holp Coporio.

The Luxembourg boys liked their own national hymn and enjoyed singing it with great harmony and gusto. One of them said the Germans offered a three thousand franc reward for the arrest of anyone caught singing it. Never a day passed but what the boys could be heard singing their anthem. It had a catchy melody and I found myself humming it and finally wrote English words to it. They insisted I sing it at our campfire gatherings and wanted copies to take home with them.

One of our sessions turned out to be a sort of carnival night. The camp comic was a little fellow also named Renee, very young and possessing an uproarious sense of humor. He and an older companion put on an act, using a dialect in both

French and German, enhanced by a sort of pantomime that made it understandable even to us Americans. We laughed until the tears streamed down our cheeks.

A little giddy from the response, little Renee put his friend and three others into a mock German infantry drill. The men were armed with shovels or sticks and he acted as a drill officer, barking out commands accompanied by crazy antics. The men did everything wrong, fell over each other and dropped their weapons. He motioned for me to come and act as inspecting officer. When he finally had them at ragged attention, he saluted me and had me review the men. The crowd howled with delight and wouldn't let us finish until two of the dummy soldiers had nearly broken each other's heads with their fake rifles. Thus passed the evening and many others, as we waited for the invasion.

Joseph was another camp character. I suppose I particularly liked him because he never rolled a cigarette without rolling one for me but he opened his heart to everyone and was always cutting wood or tending the fire. He looked more the part of a soldier than most of the rest of us and had fought with the Germans on the Russian front, where he was wounded. He had endured a severe case of trench mouth, suffered several bullet wounds and come out of it with a lame leg. He was the mechanical wizard of the camp, in charge of all bicycle repairs and knife sharpening. In addition he built a small electrical system to light our sleeping quarters by ingeniously devising a man powered generator out of an old bicycle. As long as someone was willing to pump, it produced enough electricity to power a large spotlight strung up inside. It was not the most practical of devices but it nicely served our needs. He displayed his sense of humor by erecting a fence around his invention and put up a sign that read, "Centrale Electricite, 10,000 volts, Danger de Mort."

When we had been in the camp several days, the chief of

all the area Partisan camps put in an appearance. He was a tall heavy set man and had a very dark complexion and a bushy black mustache. We four Americans shared the common desire to get back to England, so I was elected to talk to him. He was a middle aged individual who seemed amiable enough at the beginning of our conversation but, as we talked, I began to realize that he wanted us to stay with the Partisans until the invasion. It was a possibility I hadn't considered and it made me hot under the collar. I felt they had been keeping something from us. We were little more than hostages. Somehow they felt that having us would add legitimacy to their operation when the Allies came.

The more we talked, the hotter I got. Coupled with my frustration, this duplicity made me madder than hell. Finally I told him that we would wait here until the following week and that was all. When he told me he would have to go to Brussels to make arrangements, I reiterated my ultimatum. If nothing was forthcoming by then, we would leave. The chief sensed that I meant business and, while I didn't know what we would be getting into, we would at least be doing something to help ourselves. I believed I had made our position clear and felt considerable satisfaction for having spoken out.

House like Fairon house in Luxembourg

The Raid

Whether the chief would return with escape plans was questionable. Tense and impatient, I volunteered to accompany the Partisans on a Nazi raid, being motivated more by curiosity than any desire to help. The raid agreed upon was to be carried out against a suspected Nazi family who was giving a big wedding party for a daughter. Since the wedding dinner was to be held on a Saturday night, we would raid the place on the Friday night before. It would be a gala occasion, for there was sure to be lots of good food, cakes and champagne.

Just before dark on Friday the little band started out. Johnny Wieseckel had agreed to go along too and the whole party from our camp was to meet some others at the new camp. Excitement mounted at the other camp when they discovered that the Russians, the new Belgian and we two Americans would accompany them. To them it must have seemed like an international espionage party and to put sanction on the whole unpleasant business. However, it was an impressive little gathering and everyone was in high spirits, especially the Russians. This was their chance to get new clothes.

The walk to the bride's house was a long one, about twenty kilometers. My shoes, which were a size too large for me, had gotten damp from a recent rain, and I felt large blisters on my heels and toes by the time we arrived. It was past midnight. The chief signalled everyone to be quiet and I noticed several gripping their guns a little tighter. Each man was also instructed to put a handkerchief around his face to prevent the family from recognizing him later. I wondered what possible harm a bridal party could do to thirty men armed with knives and odd guns.

The chief and a couple of cohorts were now cutting the glass windows on the lower floor. We could hear occasional noises coming from inside; no doubt the family was making final arrangements for the next night's party. The glass, released from the frames, fell inward with a shattering crash. At the same moment, the leader went through a window and I could hear him giving loud voiced commands, something like "Hands up!" Then it was time for the main party to break in the door, an action that was also done with willful destruction. Then the raiders began sacking the place.

I walked in to get a better view of things. There, to my utter astonishment, were five young pretty girls standing in their nightgowns, wild eyed with fear and sobbing to see such a nightmarish sight. Their old mother and father stood by bewildered, not seeming to understand just what was taking place or what to do about it. Through a door into the living room I could see a table beautifully set for the wedding, with all the pretty dishes and glassware perfectly placed for a large number. This was not a well to do family and they had probably dug deep into their savings to throw this one great party. It struck me as brutal to see these masked men breaking open cupboards, throwing the contents out on the floor and stealing even the most personal belongings of the little family—Germans or not. This was nothing more than common burglary, even if it was a Nazi family.

Theo came out wearing a woman's hat jauntily and holding a dainty wristwatch by the strap and I immediately disliked him for it. Some were putting potatoes, bread and hams into buckets to carry back to camp. Two men came out of the basement carrying a whole case of old wine, undoubtedly a great luxury for this family, while another came up drinking a bottle of beer and letting the foam splash on the kitchen floor. The Russians came from upstairs, where they had found clothes to replace their older garments, one wearing a new suit and shoes, the other sporting an overcoat and hat. The oldest girl, probably the bride to be, pleaded with them not to take her father's clothes but her pleas fell on deaf ears. When one of the raiders came downstairs with a valise, no doubt filled with the clothes she intended for her wedding trip, her eyes overflowed with tears and she begged him not to take it. The chief, moved by her distress, directed the man to give it to the girl.

Only Johnny, Renee and I stood empty handed. What we had witnessed was devastating. No one was killed, or even injured, but nevertheless I felt I had been a party to a crime and I experienced an inner revulsion for the whole business and wished I hadn't joined them. It was a terrible sight to see these poor bewildered people looking on so dumbfoundedly. I am certain there was to be no more sleep in the house that night.

Every man was loaded down with loot. They had tied up the corners of blankets and filled them with everything from clothing to frying pans. They had even found a little money in the girls' purses. Someone shoved a box containing the wedding cake at me, something I felt represented the joy and light heartedness these people expected the day to bring. I tried to convince myself that the Nazis had it coming to them and that it was either we or they that must eat or sleep comfortably, but I could not. Our survival certainly didn't depend on stripping these poor people of their food, clothing and bedding.

Leaving the stunned and stricken family behind us, we moved off into the night. I carried the wedding cake almost reverently, knowing in the back of my mind that all too soon the sugary confection would fill the greedy guts of the raiders. I wanted no part of it.

The hike back with our heavy loads was worse than when we were empty handed. We pushed on, without stopping to rest, until the chief motioned us to follow him to a deserted farm house, where he had arranged to store the loot until the next night. We were still nearly five kilometers from camp and it was almost morning. Even without the load I had been carrying, I was stumbling with exhaustion. When we were at last at camp, I crawled in our bunk and slept until noon.

While sharing a late breakfast, I asked what was to be done with all the stuff we had stored in the old house. The answer brought forth mixed emotions. The things had been returned, for it was learned the family was not Nazi after all; they were "Belgian Partisans!" I was happy that at least some of the carnage was undone, but nothing would make good the breakage or the loss of little personal treasures and keepsakes that would never be returned, the ruined wedding that had been so carefully planned and the emotional scars those people would carry for the rest of their lives. It was another example of what happens when the facts aren't straight. They were also to be given some sort of money reparations to help cover their material losses. The chief found it a mighty embarrassing situation to be in. We found the Belgian, Renee, looking very thoughtful, for the raid had been carried out against his people.

At the end of our second week, disaster seemed imminent when the guard came pounding in and breathlessly announced that two hundred or so Germans were within a few hundred meters of the camp. It may have been the same fellow that cried alarm at the other camp; at any rate, we were galvanized into action. We hadn't had meat for several days but another raid on some farmer's herd had produced the makings for hamburgers. Already keen appetites were being whetted by the smell of cooking meat.

Renee had been in the middle of cutting my hair when the interruption came. Leaving me half shorn, he began barking orders for evacuation. By the time I had grabbed my coat and other belongings, most of the men were gone. I had a tremendous urge to snatch some of those delectable hamburgers sizzling on the stove, but discretion dictated a hasty retreat. The Germans could be closer than expected and there was no time to find something in which to carry the hot meat.

The whole crew was dashing headlong through the forest with no regard for silence. Joe Kerpan, about half way through the pack, put on an extra burst of speed and in record time was even with the leader. Any indication of danger always triggered a wild-eyed response from Joe. When we had reached a heavily wooded section with dense undergrowth, Renee secreted us there and left to scout out the situation. We heard shots coming from the direction of the other camp, indicating they were probably engaging the Germans in a fire fight. Renee whistled his return and moved us further into the woods, where we stayed until dark.

For Bob and me, this was the last straw. It wasn't much wonder this gang was being hunted like animals. The tactics they used were ruthless and it seemed they had little to do with the war effort. In fact, they were now taking large amounts of money for no other reason than to have it for their own personal use after the war. We had accepted food and protection from them but really didn't know what we were getting into. We hadn't known how they operated, but were now feeling they were no better than a gang of outlaws. Some of them were heedlessly flaunting themselves in public. One had actually stolen an automobile and hadn't had it twenty four hours, when it broke down on a public road. He was trying to get the vehicle going again, when the Nazis apprehended him. During his flight, they fired on him and he narrowly escaped with his life.

We four Americans had no stomach for what was going on. We were anxious to be on our way and felt there surely would be good people along the way who would give us food and shelter. The attitude of the big chief who had stalled us off was another deciding factor, since he hadn't returned from Brussels and the excuse given by some of the others was that the Allies were bombing the area and the train service was disrupted. It might have been true but we had reason to believe otherwise.

While we were waiting for things to settle down following this latest German scare, we made plans to escape. A little goggle-eyed Luxembourg boy whom we called the Cantonnier because of the cap he wore, wanted to go with us. Renee returned with the news that the danger had passed; the whole thing was a false alarm. What we were told was that the guard had seen a cow moving through the trees and had invented the story, but the fabrication had no ring of truth to it. There was no explanation of the shots we had heard and it only served to add weight to our decision to leave. We would wait two more days and, if there was no word from the chief, we would slip away.

The next day Renee decided to post a twenty four hour guard. That meant each of us would have to put in a stint about every other day, assuming the orthodox army method which called for two hours on and four hours off. During one of my two hour posts, another fellow, also named Joe, served with me. He was a huge teddy bear type fellow, rather simple, child-like and good natured. He had overheard some of our talk about leaving, distrusted us and took every scrap of information back to Renee. He was boring the hell out of me with snapshots and descriptions of his very large family back in Luxembourg, so, as an excuse to get away, I told him I'd walk down the line and do some scouting. When I wandered further and was gone longer than I planned, I guess Joe thought I might be up to some funny business. On my way back I met him and Renee coming along very determine faced, and Renee proceeded to tell me that it was not a good idea for

The Raid

me to leave camp so far. I merely laughed at his hidden meaning; nevertheless, I knew the Partisans were skeptical of us now.

Another raid was planned for that night but when they asked us Americans to participate, we declined. Renee hesitated when he heard our decision to stay in camp. He was no doubt reluctant to leave us behind alone but couldn't actually force us to go along. Once the raiding party had left, I hunted up Johnny Wieseckel. "Would you be willing to leave tonight?" I asked, knowing almost for certain that he would.

"Sure," he replied enthusiastically. "What do you have in mind?"

"Well, we have to talk Bob and Joe into going with us. If they stay behind, they'll face a difficult situation. That bunch of hoodlums already suspects something."

"I think we can count on them," Johnny volunteered.

Their disgust and growing impatience seemed to parallel ours but we were surprised to learn, when we told them our plan, that Bob objected. He had been ready to leave for some time and I had always been the one to hold out, thinking the big chief would surely come across with an escape plan. Then too, I took a lot of stock in Renee's assessment of our chances being slim to get across France without knowing the language, not to mention our dismal prospects of making it across the now heavily guarded borders. But, as our situation grew more untenable, I was now willing to chance it. Joe said he was ready to go anytime we were but Bob hung back.

"Well," he began doubtfully, "I don't know. I think we should wait until tomorrow."

"What the hell happened to you, Bob?" I shot back at him, irritation plainly visible. "You've always been the one campaigning to leave but I held back, thinking our chances weren't good. Now that I'm ready, you've changed your mind. How come? I'm sick of this whole setup. Johnny and I are ready to leave."

"Well then, you and Johnny go on ahead. Joe and I will leave tomorrow," he answered.

"No," I tried to spell it out for him, "it wouldn't do for us to split up. Our chances will be better with four of us. I'd rather wait until you are ready."

About that time, Big Joe, the fellow I'd served guard duty with, began hovering around where we stood in the dark. "Look" I whispered, "they've even left a guard to see that we don't leave." There was nothing left to do but go to bed, though I wondered if the big goon would actually stop us if we took a notion to go.

The next morning, the raiders returned with their booty. They had made off with a tremendous amount of loot. There were clothes of every description, new shoes, tobacco, soap, honey and various other luxuries. It looked as though they had raided a department store, skimming off all the scarce items. The various head men sat around a table and counted the money they had taken. Word was passed that it totalled more than 30,000 francs, more money than most of them had ever seen in one lump sum. It was plain that it was going to be a source of trouble, as there was dissension over how it was to be split. I was more than a little perturbed. The so-called Partisan bunch had left behind their avowed status of freedom fighters and now were nothing more than profiteers. It wasn't much wonder they wanted to keep us here to act as a reason for their existence. When the Allies came, they could say, "See, we rescued your men, saved them from the enemy." When it was all over, they would go home with money in their pockets. They had never really faced the enemy; it was just all a big callous adventure to them and it made me sick.

Bob was also disturbed by what was going on. We began to study our maps, for we needed to familiarize ourselves with the route we hoped to take and have contingency plans, if we had to detour. Our activity didn't escape Renee, the Belgian, and while he couldn't speak a word of English, he was able to make us understand that he knew all too well these men were not what they pretended to be. They were preying on his people and he wanted to leave himself, but knew they wouldn't let him go, for fear he would inform the Nazis of their activities. Knowing that we intended to leave, he cautioned that it would be difficult, with all the odds against us, but with a lot of luck we might make it.

France At Last

At five o'clock I came off guard duty. The four of us had decided to keep right on with the usual camp activity until then. We weren't entirely certain that we would by physically restrained from leaving but, not wanting to take any chances, we had kept our actual plans to ourselves. It seemed a little ridiculous that these men who had befriended us would do us any harm, but there had been many little incidents that indicated they viewed us as sort of "money-in-the-bank," so to speak. It may have been that they thought we would give them away if caught and they warned we wouldn't get five kilometers from camp before being apprehended.

Putting all the negative possibilities aside, we made up our minds to go and, fortunately, most of the men were away from camp. The few who remained, including Renee, were sleeping off their fatigue from the raid. We woke them to say goodbye and strangely, seeing our determination, they offered little objection. Renee grunted with disgust. When I invited him to visit me in the States some day, he mumbled something to the effect that I had about as much chance as a snowball in hell of getting there.

When we had gathered up our gear and reached the edge of the camp area, Renee, the Belgian, was there to meet us. Putting a finger to his lips, he motioned for us to follow him and he led us to a thick clump of trees some distance from camp. He halted us there and, in answer to his soft whistle, a whistle sounded from within. It turned out to be a young

Belgian farmer who had been bringing Renee eggs and occasionally a piece of meat. The two Belgians talked confidingly and we were all given a couple of eggs apiece. They showed us how to tap the end and suck out the contents. None of us had ever eaten raw eggs before, but the need for nourishment overcame our reluctance, and we gulped them down. I found mine hard to swallow but I supposed, like oysters, the taste had to be cultivated.

It was with mixed feelings that we said goodbye to Renee. As we started out, the sun was getting low but, with Spring in the air, we expected it to be a balmy evening. We were all in high spirits and agreed that we were glad to be on our way, regardless of the outcome. We had planned to walk the thirty kilometers to the French border by midnight and cross over under cover of darkness. Two pieces of black bread in my pocket was the only food among us but we figured that, once in France, we could find help again from Partisans.

We must have made a strange procession, for we wore a conglomeration of clothing that didn't type us either as Belgians or Frenchmen. Even if they had, they would have divided us into classes not ordinarily seen together. Bob and I still had on the business suits we had been given in Luxembourg and we carried overcoats in this warm weather. Joe had on a loud sport suit, just fine for a vaudeville act, but he also carried a raincoat. He also had a soft felt hat, while Bob and I wore caps, but most Belgian and French wore berets. Johnny Wieseckel wore the only outfit among us that would not be too conspicuous, but he had on a pair of rubber shoes which were a strange item around the countryside. We looked like neither business men nor farmers and drew curious glances from the people we encountered.

When we had left the camp about five kilometers behind, we reached a main line railroad which we had to cross to keep on our desired course. We cautiously crept through a grove of small trees to a place that offered a commanding view in both directions. At this point my heart leaped into my throat. There, not fifty yards from us, was a guard on duty. We started to move off in another direction to get around him but he saw us and kept peering in our direction, as we made our way through the underbrush. There was nothing else to do but keep going. We would have to chance it, so struck out boldly across the tracks. I was close enough to see a badge on his hat, but he wasn't wearing a uniform and didn't carry a gun that I could see. We dared not glance back to see if he followed us, though I expected him to shout a command to halt. Once on the other side, we dived into the woods and wasted no time getting clear of the area.

The prophecy of the camp Partisans had nearly come true. There was a sort of smug satisfaction in having crossed the five kilometer mark. Every kilometer we put behind us now would be a small triumph.

Our intention was to work our way South and West between the towns of Recogne and Newchatel, in an effort to reach the French border by the targeted time. Once across the border, we felt we could make our way South to Spain, missing the most heavily populated areas. We knew the Germans had used Newchatel as a headquarters. We were more than a little uneasy when we found we were passing so close to the outskirts. We weren't stopped, however, and the only people we met on the highway gave us a friendly "Bon Jour."

As twilight deepened and stars began to appear in the night sky, we passed through the small village of Bertrix. From one of the houses near the center of town we could hear the dit-dit-dah, V for Victory introduction to the "London Calling" radio program, a program prohibited in occupied countries. We concluded the Germans must not be monitoring this district very closely. On the farther outskirts of town we could see the lights of Bouillon which had a railroad to lead us directly to the

French border. About this time, a man on a bicycle passed by us, eyeing us suspiciously. He said something in French which, for lack of understanding the language, we had to ignore. After this we felt it more prudent to leave the main highway and catch the railroad at a point farther South.

We finally reached the railroad at another small village and crossed over it on a viaduct, just as a train passed underneath. When we had walked a short distance along the railroad, we heard voices coming from a deep gulch, so we were again forced to alter our plans and try going cross country by compass.

We came to a small road going in the right direction, so decided to follow it. We had been walking steadily for eight hours and each of us was beginning to feel the effects. A stinging pain in one heel informed me in no uncertain terms that a blister had broken. The others stopped while I tried to ease the problem. In the dark I couldn't see much, but I changed my sox around and folded a scrap of paper to put in my shoe, thinking it would change the pressure point. Nothing seemed to help. Finally Johnny suggested I try his rubber shoes and he would wear mine. The soft counter and cushioned soles did help and we trudged on. Little did we know at that point that those shoes were going to play a big part in our flight to safety.

While we were sitting at the roadside, we hadn't kept our voices down and I had even lit a match to examine my foot. We hadn't seen a Nazi soldier all day and we were becoming careless. When we started walking again, we had hardly gone a hundred yards from our stopping place when we walked smack into the very edge of a military garrison. I was leading at this point, because of my impaired walking and I could see the lights shining from even rows of soldiers' barracks. Dead ahead, right in our path, was a sentry hut with lighted windows. I motioned for the rest to be quiet and take to the grass alongside the roadway. There were long moments of tenseness as we passed the hut and I felt certain the sentry would notice us. But again we passed safely and we agreed later that possibly the fact that it was a Saturday night had kept the guard from being on the alert. Up ahead we saw someone approaching with a flashlight, so we left the road and darted down a canyon where a smaller road led away from the barracks area. It was some time before we began to breathe easily again and we vowed we would never again be so careless.

Before long the canyon opened into a wide valley where the Semois River, a branch of the Meuse, flowed wide and deep. It paralleled the direction we wanted to take, so we turned upstream into a road along the bank. Bob was in the lead and after an hour we discovered we were going in the wrong direction and were circling back into Belgium with no place to cross. We were very tired and the thought of having to retrace our steps took the heart right out of us but there seemed to be no alternative. Wearily we trudged back to our entry point and took the bank road in the opposite direction for another hour to a place where the map showed a bridge.

Here again I took the lead, so my limping gait would set the pace. As best we could in the darkness, we walked a distance apart, so in case of an incident only one of us would be captured. Alone with my thoughts, I tried to imagine what I would do if the bridge was guarded. As a last resort, I figured I'd try to bribe the guard with a five hundred franc Belgian note I had, though possibility of success seemed dim. Coming to another turn in this new direction, we found, instead of the massive steel structure we had expected, a small high-arched suspension bridge flung across the river at a very narrow place. There was enough light to see that there was no one on the structure and we all crossed safely.

It was nearly four o'clock and we decided to rest and study our maps before pushing on. We discovered that the river at this point too had swung away from the French side and back into Belgium. There would be several more kilometers for us to negotiate before we reached the border. We were at the point of exhaustion and were behind the schedule we had laid out for ourselves, but knew it was imperative to make the crossing under cover of darkness.

Getting up slowly, we took off downstream again on this, the opposite bank from the one we'd been walking, and kept on until we spotted a side road leading in the direction of France. We decided to chance it, but in a short time discovered we were in a valley with a high sheer bluff blocking the French side and thought we had again taken a wrong route. We simply couldn't turn back now so continued on. A little distance further, we came upon a high wire fence paralleling the road on the French side. Strangely enough, there was a gate. It seemed as though it had been placed there just for our use. This just had to be the French border. How could we be so lucky? We slipped through to the other side in seconds.

With the first real encouragement we'd had since leaving camp, our flagging spirits were lifted, and we easily scaled the cliff that had daunted us moments before. It was light when we reached the top and there, stretched out before us, were the green rolling hills of France. In spite of the circumstances, I was thrilled at the sight, even knowing that it was occupied by the Germans. I had never imagined coming into the country from this direction. My mind had always focussed on the traditional entry through a channel port. We celebrated by standing on the brink of the canyon, sharing the two pieces of bread I had in my pocket and joking about how we had fooled the Partisans. We had escaped capture up to now and, while the immediate future was uncertain, at least we were standing on French soil.

The novelty of being in France soon wore off when we began travelling again, however, and the going became increasingly difficult. We each had blistered feet by now and the blister I had broken was paining me a good deal, for it was a raw open sore. In addition, we were hungry, dirty and tired. The scraps of bread had only served to whet our appetites. As ravenous as we were, we felt that we must distance ourselves from the border, where there were sure to be enemy patrols, so we kept pushing on. We came to a small stream, where we stopped to wash and tidy up as best we could, even took off our shoes and soaked our feet in the cool water. Somewhat refreshed, we headed out in a direction we hoped would take us to the East of Sedan. From there we expected to travel South, directly toward Spain. But tall brick smokestacks along a main line railroad, which converged with our course from the West, forced us to do a lot of circumnavigating to avoid the industrial areas that would certainly be there. We kept having to zigzag back and forth, in order to dodge the numerous little towns that blocked our course, and added many unnecessary miles to our journey. It was impossible to keep a straight course due South.

After circuiting five or six towns, we began to grow despairing of our chances of making any good headway in this method. We decided we would have to take a few chances and go directly through some of the smaller towns. Certainly it wasn't a wise decision, but our hunger and fatigue were giving us a false sense of boldness which resigned patience and good judgment. To make matters worse, we had tried to get a handout at a cottage along a little travelled road and had been refused. They may have thought we were masquerading Germans or, if we weren't, we could implicate them, should we be caught. Only at one place had a man had courage enough to slip us each a piece of bread and a small slice of bologna through his back door. It was indeed the thought of going hungry which caused us to decide on taking desperate chances.

We hadn't any more than decided upon our plan of going

through the smaller towns, when one loomed up ahead. It was about the hour for going to church on this Sunday morning, so we felt that it would be safe to pass through. Everything went well until we arrived at the outskirts of the town, but there we encountered a sentinel's post with a gate directly in front of us. It was too late to turn back without drawing attention. Johnny and I were in the lead and, as we approached the post, we reached a cross street. We made a right turn into the street, as if it had been our intention all along and walked on casually. It was a close call and fear added a few extra tremors to our legs, already shaking with fatigue.

Some of the church bound people had eyed us with curiosity, so we decided to hole up at the earliest possible moment. The only place we could find was a hedgerow that edged a farmer's pasture. We pushed our way into it as far as possible and settled ourselves for some much needed sleep, only to discover that there were patches of nettles growing at the base of the prickly bushes. To add to our discomfort, it began to rain.

Sleep eluded me. After about an hour in the hedgerow, I began to grow restless and was increasingly conscious of my hunger. I turned to Bob, who was also wide awake and chewing on a blade of grass meditatively. "Let's shove off. This is for the birds."

"Okay. Wake up Johnny. I'm ready," he said, without the slightest expression. I went over and shook Johnny. He was a mess. His face and hands were covered with little white welts. He had rolled into the nettles and was too tired to notice. Leaving the town behind us, we travelled several more kilometers before we found a lonely house where we dared ask for food. I was elected to do the talking. I rapped on the window of a door a few times and finally an old man came.

"Promenade beaucoup kilomet. Fatigue. Manger s'il vous plait." That was every bit of French I could muster. I accompanied it with gestures, hoping he would understand. Our need was patently obvious but the old fellow was absolutely terror stricken. His eyes wide with the fear the Germans had instilled in every householder, he motioned us away and slammed shut the door.

We trudged on for another five kilometers and entered the town of Mouzon, where people were on their way to afternoon church services. It was no longer raining but we were dirty, scruffy, unwashed and looked a sorry sight compared to the villagers in their Sunday best. We crossed a main line railroad that passed through the town and then to the Meuse river, where we realized that we had once more miscalculated the location of a bridge. Feeling like bumbling fools, we were forced to retrace our steps through town. As we walked along the river bank, we came upon an unsuspecting young couple who were making passionate love in a grassy spot. It seemed incongruous that such a basic elemental force should be alive and well when the rest of the world was in such a turmoil and we were part of it. It reminded me of a time back in the States when I saw a poor old bum pass by a restaurant window, while I was inside enjoying a tender steak.

We slipped through the freight yards that bordered the river and from there to the bridge, which we crossed undetected. A Nazi airman on a bicycle pedaled by and took more than a passing glance at us. We had been travelling on reserve energy for some time and by now were running on empty. It was a struggle to put one foot past the other and we were so foot sore we were literally walking on the sides of our feet.

"That next town up there is as far as I can go unless we can get some food," I gasped, hoping the others would agree. I hated the others to thing I was a namby-pamby, but I had reached a point where I didn't care.

Joe said, "What took you so long? We thought you'd never give up."

As we neared the little town, we saw a huge concrete pillbox which evidently the French had intended to use against the Germans in the early part of the war. It was empty, so Bob and Joe stayed there while Johnny and I left in search of food. We tried several houses in and near the village, but were turned away empty handed. They couldn't be moved, even with the few French francs we had. Discouraged, we headed back to the pillbox. As we crossed a field, I spotted a mound, the kind farmers make to store potatoes and root vegetables. This one held rutabagas. I unearthed one and carted it to where the others were waiting. We peeled it and sliced some of the white center, but it was so pithy and bitter that we found it almost impossible to get down. At least it filled the cavities in our stomachs. We were surprised to discover that none of us could eat more than a small piece without beginning to get sick, probably the result of nervous reaction. Maybe we were just too tired, but the few bites revived us and we decided to move on to a small town which, according to our map, was a short distance off our course.

This time we split up. Johnny and I were to take a ten minute head start and canvass the far side of the settlement, while Bob and Joe would try the near side. We could cover more territory and there would be less chance of being caught. Johnny and I finally found a farmer who was willing to sell us a couple of eggs apiece and I was so overjoyed that I gave him a twenty franc tip of Johnny's money, much to the latter's dismay.

Bob and Joe had even better luck. They found a farmer and his wife in an out-of-the-way place who invited all four of us for dinner. While there wasn't enough food to satisfy our huge appetites, it was hot and nourishing and a meal I would long remember. At the urging of these kind people, we ate every bite and washed it down with wine and beer. The wife almost cried as she watched us cram the food into our mouths, food

I am sure that what we ate was the meal they had intended for themselves and their two small children. I had never seen a more sympathetic family, but they gave no indication it was anything more than normal hospitality. It was one time when manners were forgotten, for we felt that we needed the food more than they. Bob tried to help them out a little by pushing a one hundred franc note in the lady's hand.

Once we had thanked the farmer and his wife for their kindness, we headed for a small wooded area near the town and decided to sleep until dark. We had seen a haystack about a half mile from this same farmhouse and intended making it our bed for the night. Bob, who had done most of the navigating, began scanning his maps and checking the compass.

"My God! Do you know what we have been doing all day? We have traveled almost due East. We're now nearly back to the Belgian border again."

We looked at him in open mouthed disbelief. What he said was true. We crowded around the map and he pointed to where we were. This was not the town we had taken it for but one farther East. It was the first town large enough to appear on our map and provide a check point for our progress. We were farther into France in the morning than we were right now. The border with Belgium runs Southeast and we had been slanting too far to the East.

"There has to be something wrong with this damn compass. I must have checked it a hundred times during the day." He looked crestfallen. After all, his job for our ship had been as a navigator.

"Well, at least we've got a meal under our belts," I put in soothingly. For some reason I couldn't get riled up over this mistake, for my biggest concern had been my stomach. With a full stomach I wasn't inclined to be overly disturbed at his boner.

We decided to split up in the morning. Bob and Joe thought we should steal some bicycles. That way they felt we could make better time and it wouldn't take so much out of us. At our present rate, they argued, it would take us a month to get to Spain. To be sure, none of us could be certain he'd last that long. But Johnny hadn't warmed up to the idea of stealing bicycles, so it was agreed that Bob and Joe would team up on their plan, while Johnny and I would continue our journey on foot.

At dusk the four of us headed for the haystack where we planned to spend the night. Sleeping in a haystack was quite an experience, for none of us had ever tried it before. We scooped out a hole at the base, crawled in and pulled the hay around and over us. It was a very cold night but we were snug and comfortable enough to get a good sleep and much needed rest.

The next morning, we divided up the eggs Johnny and I bought and prepared to get on our way. Johnny and I were to take about an hour's lead over the other two, so we'd be well beyond the town of Beaumont by the time they reached there. That was where Bob and Joe would try for their bikes. The parting was a bit awkward. We had been through much together and now we didn't know when we'd see each other again.

Johnny and I managed to clip off the seven kilometers to Beaumont and left the town a safe distance behind us, while Bob and Joe did their dirty work. Johnny's idea was to seek help from a Catholic priest. We heard that most of them were pro-Ally and could speak English. We intended to try in the next town where we could find a cathedral.

As we stopped to rest alongside the road leading out of Beaumont and looked back toward town, we saw two figures approaching on foot. Wouldn't you know it, they turned out to be Bob and Joe catching up with us. Not only had they not gotten bicycles, but they'd had a scary experience. They had seen an armed Nazi patrol and had to pass the two men on a narrow foot bridge. Being that close to disaster had really shaken them. They'd have to try their plan at another town ahead.

This time Bob and Joe decided to go first and we would follow in fifteen minutes. Once more we said goodbye and we watched our two friends disappear down the road. We didn't learn until much later that they were taken prisoner this very day. Whether their activity aroused suspicion in their attempts to steal bicycles, we didn't know. Others told us that bicycles were licensed like autos in America and could be easily traced.

Joe Kerpan and Bob Korth

Captured in walk across France with Don Toye

The Turning Point

On this, our third day out since leaving the camp in Belgium, Johnny and I plodded along in silence, brooding over our desperate situation. Hunger gnawed at our bellies, our feet were blistered and each step was an effort. Even if we had food and adequate foot wear, what we were trying to do was a monumental undertaking. Now our gear was in terrible shape. Johnny's rubber shoes were coming apart at the seams and required frequent repairs with the tape from his escape kit. My light dress shoes that had been provided by the Luxembourgers were so stretched out of shape that I could scarcely keep them on my feet. I had cut off the tongues to pad the heels.

We traded shoes back and forth, in an effort to change the pressure points, but blisters formed in spite of the tactic. Mine were on the top of my toes and the back of my heels. His were on the bottom of his feet, caused by perspiration inside his rubber shoes. In addition, the moisture had caused his ankles to swell badly. Some extra socks would have been a God send. With Bob and Joe gone, the enormity of it all was overwhelming. A feeling of desolation and abandonment swept over me. We were alone in this strange land with no way of knowing who was our friend and who was our enemy. Trying to fill the most basic needs was precipitating a crisis. We were literally living on the edge. The only thing Johnny and I had from which to grab moral support was each other.

The sheer morbidness of my thoughts shook me, while at the same time I realized that we would have to keep our spirits up, no matter what. Seeing a shady spot in some maples alongside the road ahead, Johnny and I got the idea at the same time to stop for a rest. After a few moments I said meditatively, "Johnny, I've been thinking. Maybe Bob and Joe were right. We're never going to get to Spain travelling like this. We've got to get some bicycles. What would you say to trying for some in the next town?" I felt our situation was that desperate.

Johnny was silent as he groped in a clump of rye grass for something to chew on. I wasn't prepared for his answer.

His level gaze held on me as he said, "If you want to, go ahead, but I won't steal." It was flat out without any garnishment.

"Well, what will you do? We can't go on like this." I was somewhat irritated by his attitude, for I felt a desperate situation required desperate measures.

In a calm steady voice he answered, "I'll just keep walking no matter how long it takes. But I won't steal." A little muscle twitched in his jaw, as he continued to hold the blade of grass in his teeth, and I knew he was dead serious.

I was being the corrupter with this little proposal and I tried to rationalize the idea, though I didn't put a voice to it. We continued to sit there as I put my thoughts together. Hadn't Johnny been on those raids with the Belgians when stealing was the motive? Weren't we at war with the Germans? Would we also stop short of killing? What about the oath of allegiance to our country we had taken?

His determination not to steal was real. I knew he couldn't be swayed and suddenly I didn't want to either. I had a new measure of the man and I admired him for his stance, no matter what the outcome.

"Okay. If that's the way it's going to be, we'll do it together, but I hope you realize that I may be the one to slow us down and it may reduce our chances."

Johnny was suddenly solicitous of my well being and obviously relieved that I would go along with him. "Oh, we can take it easy. It doesn't make any difference how long it takes. We can rest a couple days at a time, if we need to." I took note of the "we" and knew with sudden comfort that that was the way it was going to be. Even in my disappointment at the thought of no relief from this nightmare, it was as if we had each breathed a breath of fresh air and we got up considerably strengthened. At this point I was determined to keep walking until hell froze over, if necessary. Back on the road, we headed for Germont, the next town on Johnny's map.

Since leaving Bob and Joe at Beaumont, the only people we had seen were a couple of civilians driving a 1940 American International van truck and an old lady who left her bicycle at the side of the road and began picking dandelions. As we approached Germont, we could see the ever-present church steeple rising above red tile roof tops. This just might be the place Johnny was seeking. As we drew closer we were surprised to see that most of the buildings were pockmarked with shrapnel and the church belfry bore gaping holes, all showing signs of long weathering. This was not new damage. Putting two and two together, we realized this had to be from World War One shelling, a considerable blow to Johnny's anticipation of finding a priest. We were told later that some border villages had been so badly damaged that they were abandoned.

Except for a couple of shoppers, the streets were empty, but there, as if to welcome us, was a tiny cafe. Without hesitation we boldly walked in, hoping for a handout. Fortunately the place was empty except for a young waitress. She gawked at the strange apparition in front of her. She couldn't understand our pidgin French until I finally pointed to a crust of bread on the counter and repeated the French word, "pain, pain." Her face lit up when she grasped the meaning but no bread was forthcoming. Instead, she ushered us to the window, pointed to a large sign down the street that read

"Boulangerie" and repeated the word "pain" several times.

It was plain we weren't going to make any headway with her. Fearing that we were tarrying too long, we left her and headed for the bakery sign. There were two women inside the shop buying bread. But when we saw them hand over ration stamps, we knew our chances of getting bread there were pretty slim. Nevertheless, I put on my best act after the women had departed. An elderly man had come in and was standing nearby, as I tried to communicate with the stone-faced woman behind the counter. I feigned hunger and began the usual patter about American pilots, fatigue and all, but she showed not a flicker of sympathy. To the contrary, this riled proprietress unleashed a staccato rain of menacing French, to indicate we'd get no bread from her, and fairly shrieked as she motioned us toward the door.

Suddenly the old man behind us, apparently having gathered the meaning of this weird play, pulled me to the window and, with great agitation, pointed to the recently reconstructed building across the street.

"Gestapo! Gestapo! Departe toot sweet!"

We understood his words well enough, as well as the urgency in his voice. As we turned to leave, he stayed us with a motion of his hand, then began talking to the unyielding madame behind the counter in a commanding voice. Without changing her expression, she carefully weighed out his weekly bread ration — one loaf and one slice, one kilo in all. Quickly he took it from her, then shoved it inside my coat, under my arm and hustled us toward the door. There wasn't much time to thank this kind gentleman for giving us his weekly supply of bread, but he must have seen the gratitude expressed in our eyes. He responded with a broad smile and a pat on my shoulder. Our rumbling stomachs left us with no inclination to refuse the food or to wonder what he would do to get by the week without his ration. The Germans had failed to squeeze the humanity out of him.

The Turning Point

Johnny and I fairly tip-toed out of town, putting that ominous building and its occupants behind us as quickly as possible. We expected with each step to hear a heart-stopping command "halt" and to be intercepted before we could escape the danger. We were eyed curiously by people passing us on the street and we imagined that every house had someone watching us from a curtained window. With genuine relief we finally reached the outskirts of town and sought cover in a wooded area.

In this moment of triumph Johnny took out a large knife that had been given to him back in the Belgian camp and began slicing our precious black loaf, first into six pieces, then into halves to make equal portions. Thick crusted and chewy they were and we gulped them down with relish, giving no thought to the lack of any liquid to make them more palatable. Our need had been fulfilled and we were grateful.

With hunger no longer a prime concern, our feelings of despair diminished and a conviction that tomorrow would take care of itself prevailed. If only Bob and Joe could have shared our good fortune. We missed them greatly. Of course, we had no way of knowing that they had been caught stealing bicycles and even now were on their way to prison.

According to Johnny's map, the next town on our route would be Buzancy, about an hour out. As we took off over meadows and marshes in that direction, our path brought us to a large fir forest and just inside the woods, we stumbled into a woodcutter's camp. The woodcutter and his woman with a small child huddled around the fire as they ate their dinner. This was a chance for us to get better directions and for me to beg for a cigarette. Although the old man had no tobacco to offer, he picked up a battered, smoke blackened messkit from the fire and offered it to us. It was still half filled with a sort of chicken and gravy dish, but, after one look at the thin worn features of the mother and child, Johnny and I refused. Even in their pitiful state, they apparently thought us to be in worse shape than they. At least we were happy to accept directions from them.

With Johnny's efforts to point out our proposed route to Spain on his map, the old man was able to draw a crude map on the ground for the area we were now in. It proved most helpful. There were long cleared pathways through the woods that led in the general direction we wanted to travel. After briefly thanking these people for their kindness, we began our journey down one of the corridors he had indicated. We saw on either side of us endless barbed wire entanglements woven in and around half filled trenches and log bunkers. These had to be relics of World War I. It didn't take much imagination to envision an army bivouacked here. I speculated on how the soldiers of that conflict might have felt, had they known that twenty-five years later some of their sons would be fleeing through these selfsame woods.

When we had finally worked our way through the woods, a nearly flat, open countryside spread before us. The knee I had injured in my parachute landing was protesting all the abuse I had given it. Twinges of pain shot up and down my leg and I welcomed the sight of a grassy knoll on which to flop down for a rest while Johnny studied his maps. In the late afternoon sun, I dozed off and Johnny slumped down beside me.

The village of Sommauthe was between us and Buzancy, so upon awakening and heading that way, we hoped to find it a likely place to beg for food and put up for the night. We came upon a large farm house well built and showing signs of recent repairs and fresh paint. This struck us as most unusual in this occupied country, where even the most rudimentary materials were non-existent. What was even more strange was evidence of a recent telephone installation. The place was back from the highway and well concealed. It didn't seem likely the Nazis would be here in this remote area, so we decided to take a chance. Again, the thought of a good warm meal made us bold.

Johnny was content to let me do the talking. He was extremely shy in the best of circumstances and, under these conditions, was practically tongue tied. He was more comfortable plotting our routes and prodding me to keep moving, when I was ready to give up. In answer to my knock, a rather bitter-faced elderly woman opened the door. Behind her stood a portly man in overalls. I went into my little spiel, "American soldat. Parachute. Promenade beaucoup kilomet. Donnez moi manger s'il vous plait," always accenting the last syllable in the French way, hoping they would understand me.

I was met with blank incomprehension. The lady left and came back with a plump young woman who looked as though she might be the cook or housekeeper. She gave me a cheerful "Bon Jour" in precise French. As I went through my little spiel again, still not knowing what we had walked into, I saw her face turn crimson and her hand flew to her mouth in a gesture of horror. She brushed out the door, slamming it behind her. Grabbing us each by the arm, she pulled us away from the house excitedly. As we hurried along, she pointed back at the house exclaiming "Deutsche!" and she led us panting behind a large briar thicket. Here, out of view of the house, she pointed across a plowed field to a small wood and let us know by pointing to the hands of Johnny's wristwatch that she would meet us there at six o'clock. In a mixture of French and English, she explained that the farmer who was out in the field was German and the elderly couple were his parents. Fortunately for us, they didn't understand French. No wonder she was horror stricken. She was a farm worker and would be free when she finished her chores.

We were only too eager to follow her instructions. When we were safely hidden in the wood, we kept wanting to peer out at the farm house to see if there was any sign of activity that might indicate pursuit. We wondered what the young woman would tell the old couple, if they questioned her. Our situation seemed untenable without complete trust in an unknown person. And yet, our benefactor was obviously French and certainly there had been no reason for her to take the trouble to hide us, only to betray us later. There was nothing to do but play it out.

True to her word, the young Partisan woman came back at six o'clock. She said she lived in Sommauthe and would hide us nearer her home while she went for food. The plan worked well and she returned to our new retreat with a small portion of bread, cheese, a tin of Spanish sardines and a chunk of butter. It was a brave thing for her to do and earned our heartfelt thanks. This was a real feast for us, so after warm goodbyes, we put Johnny's knife to use, this time using it as a can opener, knife, fork and spoon.

With good food lifting our spirits once again, we debated where we would spend the night. A haystack seemed the logical choice but the only one we had seen was back on the German farm. It was getting dark, a cold wind was blowing and we needed to get settled for the night, so we decided to chance it. We sneaked back to the place and burrowed into the stack. This one was damp and moldy smelling, but we had no choice. We dug in as far as we could and curled up together. The dampness penetrated our clothes and didn't help our tired muscles and aching bones, but fatigue overrode our discomfort and we slept.

Neither of us had made any religious references to the various ways we had been helped the last few days, even to being saved from our folly, but I said many silent prayers of thanksgiving and I was sure Johnny was doing the same. Already there were signs that our prayers were being answered.

Early the next morning, we crawled out of our damp hole and tried to brush the moldy mess off our clothes. I ached in every bone and had become feverish, although Johnny appeared to be in better shape. I had been wearing his rubber shoes the day before and now the bottoms of my feet were like two large boils from the sweating. It was only through his coaxing that I was able to start out, for the needle piercing pain at every step was unbearable.

I hobbled along behind Johnny and we reached Buzancy about nine o'clock. Because it appeared too imposing a place to walk directly through on the main road, we circled around it until we were again heading South toward Spain. A mile or so from the town's outskirts, we cut across some farmers' fields and converged on a small stream working its way restively through heavy stands of alder on either bank. This being an excellent place for concealment, Johnny and I dropped wearily on the bank to wash the grime from our faces and hands and to soothe our aching feet in the water. I had reached another low ebb in spirit and felt I should level with Johnny.

Apologetically I began, "Johnny, Spain is a whole month away. I don't think I can make it. Why don't you go on alone? I'll just be a burden to you. I'll try to get some help and stay here until my feet get better."

He brushed off the idea. "Nawh, we'll make it okay. We can hide right here for awhile. I can scrounge for food and after a couple days you'll be in better shape." I appreciated his continued use of "we". He told me much later that he had feared at this point that I might give myself up to the Nazis.

Before I could answer him, we were suddenly interrupted by a sing-song chant in cadence, evidently from a large group of marching men now approaching us along the opposite bank. The tone was weirdly plaintive like the song of a prison gang. As they drew closer, their song reached a higher pitch, almost a frantic wail, a ghastly song of crazy men. Then there were flat voices with authority of men who seemed to be pressing this group from the rear. The wailing chorus enveloped us completely, as their troop crossed our hiding place on the opposite bank and Johnny and I crouched low. As they passed by, we could see that many of them wore army greatcoats like the British issue and there was a hodgepodge of army tunics, trousers and shoes, mostly baggy and worn. The explanation for all this was revealed to us, when two huge swarthy looking men wearing white turbans brought up the rear. This was the dress of soldiers from India and they were exercising a contingent of prisoners from their own country. The whole lot had no doubt been taken prisoners by the Germans at Tobruk or El Alemain in the North African campaign. One of their men, obviously a British non-com acting as patrol leader, passed close enough to see us but gave only a slight nod that he was aware of our presence and never broke step. There were about fifty men in the bunch and most likely a Nazi non-com somewhere in the rear. We decided to abandon our hiding place and seek another, for surely there would be German guards shepherding these prisoners of war.

In order to avoid running into this group of prisoners again, we had to retrace our steps back toward Buzancy. From the outskirts of town, luckily, we found a paved highway heading in the Southerly direction we were taking. Knowing that we were still close to the area where we met the prisoners and having hardly well started on this new course, we were startled when a powerful black sedan careened around the curve behind us and sped past us. Three officious looking men, not uniformed, cast curious looks at us, as they sped by, but we feigned disinterest. There was little doubt in our minds that these suspicious looking burlies, driving an official looking car in a land where private cars were almost nonexistent, were V.I.P.'s of the Third Reich.

There were open fields on either side of us, but Johnny and I felt we had to stay on the road in order to avoid looking suspicious. The car soon disappeared from sight ahead of us.

The Turning Point

A half mile down the road we rounded a bend and there, just a quarter mile ahead, sat the big black sedan, facing us and blocking our way. The pounding of my heart shook me from head to toe. We were sure they were the enemy and had stopped for the sole purpose of arresting us. Recognizing the futility of putting up any resistance, within a few seconds I calmed down and prepared to meet whatever fate awaited us.

"Well, Johnny, it looks like this is it. At least we lasted longer than the five kilometers they gave us credit for back in camp," I admonished bitterly.

"Yeah, it looks pretty bad," Johnny replied with a sigh.

We began tearing up our fake Belgian passports. If we were to be taken prisoner, we would claim our American identities. We let the pieces trickle from our fingers, as we walked along the roadside.

"Guess the best thing to do is to walk right into them, as if we had nothing to hide," Johnny whispered resignedly.

We walked along silently and I wondered what life in a German prison camp would be like. I also wondered what fate might have befallen Joe and Bob and whether we had been wise in leaving the Partisan camp back in Belgium. After all, I had been largely responsible for urging the others to make the attempt. In my recollection of this crisis, it seems to me that Johnny and I exchanged a few words of parting, so sure were we that this was the end.

As we came into plain view of the sedan, I could see only one occupant, the driver, an unusually large man. At the side of the road were two of the British uniformed prisoner guards that we had seen with the work gang. The two other occupants of the car were standing with them, conversing together. When the Indians of the work force came into view in a marshy strip alongside the road, they were cutting some sort of long plant stalks growing in the boggy ground.

It suddenly occurred to me that just possibly the two in

street clothes, talking to the prisoner guards were there expressly for some kind of business involving the work detail and not interested in us at all. Could it be that we were completely wrong in our assessment of the situation? The two men from the car were busily talking to the guards and paid no attention to us at all. The driver of the car eyed us curiously as we walked by and Johnny and I scarcely dared to breathe. Could it be that they weren't going to stop us? We kept an even slow gait in passing and pretended to be talking to each other disinterestedly. At every step, we expected to hear the command "halt," but none came. We were approaching a curve in the road ahead and would soon be out of view.

As we rounded the curve, we came to a bridge crossing the same stream the prisoners had been working and large patches of bulrushes grew at each abutment. As soon as we were certain we were out of sight, we jumped off the road and scrambled for cover along the stream bank, hardly daring to believe our good fortune. We were safe, for the moment at least.

Time passed and it seemed that the danger was over. Johnny and I edged closer to the stream to soak our feet once again. The sun filtering into our hiding place played no favorites, for it warmed us as well as our enemy and our spirits began to rise again. My feet oozed with happiness in the mud and my body began to respond to the warmth of the sun. The recent danger gradually faded from our minds and we spent long minutes in silence watching the stream ripple by. The conflict seemed far away and it was hard not to be lulled into complacency.

As the cool water gradually removed some of the heat from my swollen feet, my attention began to focus on the Spring awakened world around me. The birds and bees, frogs and other crawling things were everywhere but they were totally unaware of the man-made turmoil a few miles away. How odd it seemed that most often it is God's wild creatures in the biological chain that are out fighting their battle for survival. In our contemplation of nature, a cat may pounce on a mouse, a robin may catch a worm, or a frog may snatch a fly and it is just the natural order of things. These predators are merely following their instincts. What is not so natural is man hunting man, hell bent on his destruction—especially when his enemy may be a total stranger, though possibly of the same blood.

During the Civil War in the States, it is said, there was brother against brother. Was this conflict so much different? Maybe we weren't actual blood brothers, but we belonged to the same brotherhood of man. It was strange that these thoughts should intrude on this idyllic scene. They brought to mind a story I had heard concerning the crew of an American bomber that had been shot down. They had been taken prisoner by the Germans and were being transported to prison by train. Irate crowds in the German cities along the way threatened to lynch them. They screamed epithets, beat on the sides of the coach and called them murderers, whereupon one of the guards handed his pistol to one of the Americans and told him to use it against the mobs of his countrymen if necessary. How easy it was to switch roles.

Downstream from us, the current slowed, spreading its waters into a fifty foot wide morass. Here, someone, probably the prisoner work crew, had placed numerous bundles of wood stalks crosswise in the stream for soaking. So many had been placed that a man could ford the stream at several points without wetting his feet. We had no idea what they were to be used for. In these war torn countries they had to make use of everything.

Johnny nudged me and placed his finger to his lips for silence to signify that somebody was approaching. A fat, dark skinned man, wearing a British Army greatcoat and a tan army overseas cap, was moving along on the opposite bank. His gold rimmed glasses glinted in the sunlight. It turned out he was looking for a place to relieve himself. He stopped directly across from us, took off his heavy coat, carefully folded it on the grass, slowly pulled down his trousers, and poised himself like a football quarterback, as he began his toilet. We watched in stony silence, as a pleased expression crossed his face, and he began feeling around for something to complete the ritual, much as a cat scratches for soil to cover his excrement. He finally pulled bunches of grass and, when he was satisfied, pulled up his trousers, unfolded the greatcoat and put it back on with the same meticulous attention he had when he took it off. Shrugging his shoulders, he adjusted his glasses and sauntered back in the direction of his comrades. In the next hour we were not disturbed again, except that we sighted an old woman across the stream gathering dandelions.

Toward noon another one of the prisoners had worked his way over near the same spot where the black man had done his toilet. To my surprise, this man was quite fair and bore an amazing resemblance to Bing Crosby, our American crooner. This man carried a mattox dangling from an arm on one side. Over his shoulder he carried the typical musette bag, which no doubt contained his lunch, and a wine bottle stuck out from under the flap. He was dreamily watching the bundles lying crosswise in the stream.

Johnny and I sat like statues. We could have spit on him, we were so close. Perhaps the intensity of my gaze caused him to turn and look directly into my eyes. For a second he stood motionless. If he should sound an alarm, we would be lost. I took the bold approach and motioned for him to come across. He understood and, without saying a word, crossed one of the rows of bundles to stand before us. Using the sort of universal language we had become quite good at, Johnny and I explained our situation. He readily began to sympathize with us.

From his mixed words, we gathered that he was "Polonnaise" and that he and his family had been transplanted here to harvest this wood fibre for making matches and ersatz clothing. When he saw the condition of my feet, he eyed my shoes and offered to exchange with me. His were the conventional high tops like our own G.I.'s, but they were much too small for either Johnny or me to wear. With much compassion our new friend made it clear that he would be back later, bringing us food and bandages. With that he departed hastily.

It seemed only a few minutes had elapsed, when we began receiving visits from every Polonnaise and Czech in the area. We learned that there were several transplanted families in the community. As soon as one group arrived, another would congregate in an inconspicuous place and await their turn. The first group was Czech, with one old fellow acting as spokesman for all these conscripted foreigners. They all lived with as much of their families as they could bring with them in a single section of the prison community. They worked pretty much apart from the African prisoners. The old Czech had a teenage son who told us his father had a short wave radio and all the exiles came secretly to listen to "London Calling." He said there had been another bomber pilot who had landed near here. He was badly injured and the people here had taken care of him in this self-same spot. A wonderful feeling enveloped us as we felt the security of their friendship. Each group promised to return with supplies.

It wasn't long before our first friend returned, accompanied by another Pole and his Czech friends. They brought food, clothing and bandages. These was hot gruel, pork fat, bread, cheese and wine. Someone had even contributed a bottle of beer. We ate greedily and drank until we were dizzy. Our friends advised us to stay another day to rest up and we agreed that it would be wise.

With clean socks over my bandaged feet, I began to feel that maybe I could make it to Spain after all. Again Johnny and I agreed that God had arranged this good fortune. We had twice been saved from almost certain capture in the last twenty four hours. It was also becoming apparent to me that Johnny's Christian refusal to steal bicycles had not only prevented any pursuers from having means for tracing us, but it had also provided the excuse for our stumbling into this haven of rest. Also we could pray unabashed without feelings of guilt.

Our new friends provided us with a plain but tasty dinner and returned at dark to lead us to a haystack where we could hole up for the night. This time it was fine dry hay. We burrowed and slept through the night warm and secure. In the morning our friends joined us at the stream bank and brought eggs and wine for breakfast. The old Czech asked to see Johnny's map and pointed out the location of a German airfield just a mile away. His gnarled old finger pointed out spots that we should avoid. Then, seemingly as an afterthought, he queried of Johnny, "Vous promenade... marche?" and he pointed to the map with circular motions, wanting to know where we were heading.

"Spain, Spain," Johnny replied, unfolding another map to show him how our route would take us to the country South of France.

"Non, non, non," the old man rattled off. "Allemand ist caput."

After several attempts, he made us understand what had been hinted back in Belgium. The underground escape lines had been intercepted by the Germans. No one was getting through to Spain. He explained that Patriots, attempting to take downed Allied pilots across the Pyrenees, had been shot and all routes were heavily guarded. He explained further that, for a while, the French had been able to get some of our people through by disguising them as sheepherders. The Germans had discovered the ruse and now it was out of the question.

"Suisse, Suisse," the old Czech repeated, pointing to the map. "Kilomet petit. Un avion part d'Angleterre," meaning that an airplane would take us from there back to England.

The Turning Point

He measured on the map to show that Switzerland was just one third the distance to Spain. We had some reservations about the idea of a plane taking us to England, but it did seem possible that the Swiss might bend their neutral position enough to give us haven, especially since the invasion was imminent.

I was easily convinced of the feasibility of the move. With my feet in such poor condition, the shorter route would be most welcome and Johnny agreed. The only reason we hadn't considered Switzerland was the fact that back at the base we had heard stories about downed airmen making it to Spain and being flown to England almost immediately. Switzerland and Sweden were places of internment. The word was that from Spain or Portugal you could get home.

As we studied the map, we realized that perhaps Switzerland was our intended destination all along. Hadn't we veered East almost from the start, especially that first day when Bob's compass was off? All along we had unconsciously been going more East than South.

So Switzerland it was to be. We looked at each other with agreement and from somewhere came the conviction that we would actually make it. Maybe these damned shoes of mine never wanted to go to Spain in the first place, but they had led us to this turning point.

No Man's Land

Our altered plans called for us to head for Montfaucon, about twenty-five kilometers distant. From there we would pass through Ardennes Forest and West of Verdun. This area had been the "No Man's Land" of the last great conflict. We had read of the terrible battles fought there and had great respect for the men who had persevered. The old Czech urged us to travel by night, so we didn't expect to see much.

At dusk our friends gathered to give us a small farewell party. They brought with them a British Army Indian soldier who had been taken prisoner by the Germans at Tobruk. Surprisingly blonde, he didn't fit our idea of an Indian soldier. Perhaps there had been an Englishman somewhere in his ancestry. He spoke little English, but fit right in with the festivities. He pulled a packet of food from his pocket and pushed it in my hand, explaining that it had been given to him by the British Red Cross. It contained a few highly prized sticks of chocolate, the first we had seen in months. Just the smell of it was enough to set our mouths watering. We thanked him profusely and, after a toast of good red wine, we said goodbye to those who had befriended us so generously. We left with the feeling that somehow this ragged multi-national group was happy they had been able to do something to outwit the Germans. They had been uprooted from their homelands, oppressed and ill used, but their pride and humanity were intact.

The long rest and nourishing food had given us renewed vigor. With well mended socks on my feet and my shoes padded in strategic places, I felt ready to tackle the next step of our journey. Perhaps we were becoming hardened to the arduous task we had set for ourselves. At any rate, we set out in high spirits. The knowledge that we were cutting the mileage by at least two-thirds also added to our euphoria.

By the time darkness overtook us, we felt quite safe walking along the deserted highway. There was no moon and, as the miles clicked off behind us, the night seemed to get darker. Only the macadam under our feet gave us a sense of direction. We practically had to feel our way along. The long finger of a church spire split the stars ahead of us, indicating we were coming to a town. Not a glimmer of light was to be seen, as we groped our way along the village streets. The town center acted like a hub and, like the spokes of a wheel, streets splayed off in several directions. We could only pick one that headed in the direction we wanted to go and hope it was the right one. We knew that the Nazis had imposed a curfew in these occupied areas and, with every step, we prayed that some barking dog wouldn't give us away.

A raw wind hit us when we left the protection of the buildings in town. In spite of increasing our pace in an effort to keep warm, we were soon shaking with cold. There was half the night remaining, but we decided to leave the road and seek protection in a grove of trees. We lay down, wrapping my thin overcoat over the both of us and placing Johnny's short coat over our heads. We huddled together to retain what little body heat we could and I clung to Johnny's back without fear of immodesty, for there was no thought of shyness in our weary condition. In spite of the intense cold, we fell into a fitful sleep from exhaustion.

In about a half an hour our limbs and joints began to stiffen and, to cap it off, something Johnny and I had eaten back at the hideout, possibly the fat pork or a sharp smelly fromage, was sickening us. Along with this, I was getting a fever and a rumbling in my stomach that announced whatever I had eaten wasn't going to stay there long. Realizing that walking would be more bearable than being still, we took off down the highway again in search of a better shelter. It was still quite dark.

We hadn't gone far when we spotted close to the road what appeared to be a calf shed. Inside we found enough material to build a small fire. We bellied up to it and finally drifted off to sleep, but not before vowing to henceforth skip night travel.

We were awakened early the next morning by the sound of someone whistling. It was a small boy, wandering aimlessly in the field near the shed. The weather was considerably improved and the feverishness I felt a few hours before had dissipated. The dysentery stayed with me but I felt well enough to travel. Johnny, in his usual style, was anxious to get going again, so we kicked dirt over the ashes of our little fire and clambered up the bank to the highway.

Now, contrary to our original plan, we would be passing through the Ardennes area in broad daylight. We began seeing signs placed on a fence that read, "Militaire Reserve. Danger de Morte." Numerous shell casings littered the ground inside the fence. There were even signs warning of gas contamination. However, we had seen no sign of Nazi takeover. About this time, a little wrinkled old man, wearing wooden shoes and with a beret clinging to the side of his head, came clopping down the road toward us. He could have stepped out of a Hans Christian Anderson fairy tale. Johnny wanted to verify the location of a town he had spotted on the map. "Esnes" was in line with our "Montfaucon" destination, so he decided to test his French proficiency by questioning the little old fellow. He was met with a blank stare, as he gave an American pronunciation to the word "Esnes." Johnny, looking somewhat abashed, pointed to Esnes on the map.

The little man's face lit up with a huge smile. "Ayne, Ayne," he said forcefully in a high pitched voice, as he pointed in the direction from which we had come.

We thanked him and continued on our way. Johnny muttered, "I'll stick to reading the map. From here on, you do all the talking."

It was about noon when we reached Montfaucon. Spring added a freshness to its appearance and it seemed more attractive than the other towns we had passed through. As we passed by a handsome brick church, a funeral service was just breaking up, judging by the battered old hearse just then hauling away the casket. Everyone was neatly dressed, considering the poverty stricken conditions of the times. Boys and girls spick and span, men and women in Sunday finery, even though this was only Thursday, all seemed to be actually enjoying a celebration in the Spring sunshine, albeit a solemn occasion. In occupied France there were obviously all too few occasions for any kind of revelry.

Mingling with the crowd were two nattily dressed French gendarmes, wearing their black uniforms trimmed in red and a big letter "S" insignia on their caps. Our Polish friends had warned that officers wearing these uniforms were commissioned by the Vichy government of Marshall Petain and held their jobs by being in sympathy with the Germans. They pulled out of the churchyard and turned into the street we were travelling.

There was no way we could blend into the crowd. Our tattered and weary appearances gave instant testimony that we didn't belong there. The two of them laughed and talked intimately, while their gait slowed to an amble. It was all we could do to stay behind them without appearing even more suspicious. Just as we came to an intersection and felt we must pass them, the city hall came into view down the side street and the two of them turned off, eyeing us curiously as they did so. Keeping a slow pace for appearances through the rest of the city streets, we were relieved at the chance to take off cross country again at the outskirts. Alone again and out of danger,

Johnny and I found walking through the countryside bathed in Spring splendor not at all unpleasant. However, we had to stop often for me to rid myself of my poisons, for regurgitating the rotten cheese and frequent calls to answer my dysentery problem which continued to hang on. I couldn't take much more without being completely wrung out. We had consumed the last of our food many miles and hours ago. We were passing through a small hamlet at the edge of Verdun, when our need forced us to try our luck at two different houses about a mile apart. Both families responded generously with eggs, bread, butter, potatoes and whatever else they could spare from their larders. Begging was entirely alien to my nature, but then there had never before been the need for it. We were becoming used to this sort of living by now and I had no fears or embarrassment in begging for our meals. We enjoyed a pleasant repast and slept fairly comfortably in a haystack near the town.

When morning came, we decided to treat ourselves to a hot meal. Yesterday's handout contained some sausage along with other makings, so it deserved a try at least. We found an old deserted farmhouse with plenty of firewood lying around, even some rusty old tin sheets that would serve as skillet and dinner plate. Once again Johnny's knife became an important utensil. After frying sausage, eggs and fried potatoes, Johnny cut slabs of bread and toasted them on the tin, then smeared them with good country butter. The best of French chefs could have done no better. Two American "hoboes" were developing a fine gourmet touch in this foreign land. All we needed was some good American coffee.

During this relaxed atmosphere, Johnny and I had been oblivious of our close proximity to the city of Verdun. As it so happened, we were encamped just around the rim of a small hill which sat on the city's Northwest boundary. Perhaps awareness of this might not have deterred us from our culinary efforts even then, what with all that beautiful food in store, but the section of the city on which we had encroached, just happened also to be contiguous to a reserve on which the Germans were practicing war games. As we started out again, unaware that we were inside the reserve and rounded the edge of the hill, we were confronted with the unmistakable sounds of the cadence of marching infantrymen and the barked commands of their officers. Since we were unable to determine the exact location of the sounds, we continued circumventing the hill cautiously.

Suddenly, as we descended upon a broad plain between the hill and the city, we located the marching columns directly in front of us. We were approaching the very area where riflemen and machine gunners were practicing trench warfare but we had not yet been observed. In our attempt to circle back West to avoid this activity, we came headlong within speaking distance of a column of marchers. Our guardian angels were certainly looking after us. The officers had in mind only the training of these raw recruits and weren't looking for American fliers, masquerading as French peasants.

To be sure, we had seen the signs indicating that the area was a military reserve, but the fences had been removed in many sections. The signs that we did see were the same as those we had seen all along the Ardennes, where everything seemed to have been abandoned. Hastening to get away, we worked our way back around the Western edge of the reserve and away from the marching troops. In doing so we crossed a large abandoned ammunition dump with a dilapidated rusty gate leading off the range. We darted through unobserved.

Once more we began our steady march toward Switzerland. Walking with full stomachs was actually invigorating and the few Spring showers that fell were refreshing. Off to our left, a tall column crowned the only hill in the broad plain we were traversing. Later we were told it was a monument to

Allied soldiers who had a famous battle there twenty-five years ago. Recalling that Adolph Hitler, after signing the 1940 French surrender in the Versailles rail car, had exhibited a fetish for wanting to eradicate old Allied landmarks, we wondered why this well-preserved monument had been left standing. After closer inspection, it occurred to us that it might make an excellent observation tower, in face of the impending invasion. The very thought of such a possibility prompted us to give it a wide berth, even though the beautifully landscaped park at its base would have been a pleasant place to visit.

Travelling through the fields and forests of the Ardennes district, avoiding towns whenever possible, we made good time and reduced the chance of a German encounter. Along the way we passed near the small village of Souilly. It was there, to our amazement, we discovered a neat two-story building. It was freshly painted white and across the front in bold black letters was the inscription, "Dedicated to the U.S. soldiers who fought and gave their lives here." A little farther on was a small white monument dedicated to a Pennsylvania Company. The grass around these monuments was fresh and green and as meticulously groomed as if it was to be used for a Bob Hope golf tournament. These memorials were in sharp contrast to the rundown conditions of the surrounding area. The French Resistance had found a way to literally thumb their noses at the Germans.

In all the swastika bedecked buildings we had seen in Luxembourg and Belgium, the intended message of triumph and power was not nearly as telling as what we were seeing here. Terrible battles were waged on this ground. It had been soaked with the blood of Allied soldiers and the French were not about to forget it. What a wonderful way to show their contempt for the oppressors and at the same time welcome the troops who would soon be coming as an invasion force. These subtle signs, so neatly maintained by the French, had somehow been overlooked by the badgered Germans and brought forth smiles of appreciation from Johnny and me.

Late in the afternoon, we dropped down from the gently rolling hill country into a narrow valley, scarcely wide enough to accommodate a country road alongside a meandering stream. As we became more accustomed to begging for food, it was a matter of routine to look for likely places, when our stomachs told us it was meal time. Our target this time was a small farm house tucked away in a wide flat spot. The farmer and his wife at first showed some reluctance to help us, but our hangdog, weary traveler's appearance won them over and they invited us to dinner.

It was a savory meal with squirrel encasserole, the usual boiled potatoes, black bread and port wine. The wine and good food loosened our tongues and our host confided that he had hesitated to invite us in, because he was employed as a laborer by the Vichy government. It was the same "C'est La Guerre" displayed by many Frenchmen who were being humiliated by the Vichy regime. He seemed somewhat relieved after the admission, though we certainly understood the position he was in. There was no reason for him to apologize for working for them. They had to survive some way and we knew, when the chips were down and the invasion in full swing, such people as these would be behind us.

Johnny and I changed the subject as quickly as possible and offered praise where praise was due. The couple relaxed and became quite jovial, as they pressed upon us eggs, bandages and medicine. They even pointed out a woodman's lean-to, where we could build a fire and spend the night. Their hospitality seemed boundless and we searched for adequate words to express our gratitude.

After a good night's sleep, we warmed ourselves with a small fire but, lacking cooking utensils, we had to eat our eggs raw in the fashion we had learned in Belgium. As we soaked up the warmth of the fire, we congratulated ourselves on how much our situation had improved. Suddenly our calm reflections were interrupted by the deafening roar of a low flying plane that buzzed our shanty and jolted us back to reality. We were still in enemy territory and safety was many kilometers away. Our re-awakened awareness moved us to quickly extinguish the fire and conceal ourselves in the forest. It was easy to imagine it was an enemy plane and, while it could have been one of our own, we didn't linger to find out.

All along the route we had travelled, Johnny had maintained a hope that we could contact a Catholic priest. He felt that we would certainly get help from the church. There were many stories in American circles of priests who had helped soldiers escape. They were believable, because there was no love lost between the Clergy and the Nazis. Except for the assistance we had been given by Father back at Bostogne, however, we'd had no success. It seemed most likely that many priests had gone underground to maintain a low profile until the end of the war.

We were now approaching a small village with a church less pretentious than most, and Johnny voiced his hope again that this might be the place. Sure enough, as we came closer, a priest fully robed and with a Bible in his hands, was pacing back and forth in front of the humble structure. Finding him completely engrossed in the Holy book, I made the first overture for Johnny by asking the clergyman if he could speak to us in English. My question was ignored, as this man, face drawn thin and unshaven, continued walking with his eyes cast down upon his open Bible. He was obviously a sick man but, under Johnny's continued pressing, he finally found words to say, "I... I...have not spoke it for so long." He seemed troubled.

Johnny was a devout Catholic and was not expecting to be put off by this figure of the church. Hoping to get a response, he asked, "Could you get us a razor for a shave?" and he rubbed his chin to add weight to his plea.

"No, no, no. We do not have," was the priest's response in jerky English.

I knew Johnny thought that asking for something as concrete and everyday as a razor might provide an opening and lead to the help we were seeking. Rebuffed by this man who was supposed to be a shepherd of the flock, he was crestfallen and perhaps a little ashamed in front of me that someone holding a church office had been so lacking in sympathy.

He turned away and we went on through the town. It occurred to me that the old priest may have been senile. Johnny remained silent, even as we stopped in a little grove of trees to eat the last of our bread and cheese. He had often said, "If we can just find a priest, our troubles will be over." The thought must have sustained him many times, giving him the strength and motivation to keep us going.

"It's Saturday. I could sure go for a bath and a good bed tonight," were the first words he said, after the disappointing encounter with the priest.

"Sounds good to me, Johnny. Let's stop early, if we can find a likely place."

"Okay, early it is," he added.

Consulting the map, we found we were near the town of Pierrefitte and soon found a place that met our criteria. It was tucked back off the forest road we were travelling. A lonely looking place, its path to the front door had so seldom been used it was scarcely discernible. Just ideal, I thought to myself and motioned Johnny to follow me. As we checked out the back of the house, we found a woman hoeing a garden and the farmer himself working in a field a little farther out.

"Bon Jour, Madame," I said politely in my best French.

"Bon Jour," she responded with seeming disinterest.

I moved closer to pat a large shepherd dog that came

bounding over from where the farmer was working. It seemed to please her that the dog trusted me. I again attempted to engage her in conversation. Pointing to Johnny and then at myself, I began my usual spiel, "American pilots. Promenade beaucoup kilomet. Fatigue." I patted my feet and adopted a downbeat look to gain her sympathy. She stopped hoeing and eyed us carefully, not showing any change of expression. About this time, a small girl came from the house and peered at us from behind her mother's skirts. I scratched the dog behind his ears and patted him briskly. He looked up at me and leaned against my leg. This seemed to delight the child and she sidled over and her small hand joined mine in petting the ecstatic dog.

With both the dog and the child vouching for us, the woman decided to be hospitable. "Vous mange?" she asked.

"Oui, oui," I answered with considerable enthusiasm.

With that exchange, she called her husband over and told him who we were. With no hesitation, he began talking excitedly about his service with the French Army during the last war, all the while moving toward the house and motioning us to follow. We had again earned our own small victory.

Once in the house, he produced snapshots of himself in uniform and proudly pointed out his medals. It was plain that the man was happy to share his opinion of the Germans and we jointly began cussing the "Hun." In typical European fashion, he called his wife and set her to work cooking for us. Out came a bottle of colorless schnapps that he had reserved for just such an occasion. There followed toasts to America and toasts to France. The potent liquor burned all of the way down, bringing tears to our eyes, loosening our tongues and heightening our laughter. It was the greatest of treats and Johnny and I tendered our "Merci, beaucoup" with convivial emphasis.

The kitchen, dining room and living room of this house were combined in one great room. A huge fireplace, wide enough for a ten foot log and tall enough for a man to stand in, took up most of one wall. A massive unpainted wood table with benches on either side was centered in the room. Against one unwindowed wall was what I had heard called a dry sink, because there was no plumbing. There was an open cupboard with shelves for dishes and utensils and beside it a large wood range.

Two bedrooms adjoined this multipurpose room, one for the family and one for an itinerant hired hand and his wife who were away for the day. A door from the family bedroom opened into the cowshed beyond and this became the main thoroughfare at milking time. If Johnny and I were to get the bath we had hoped for, it would have to be with water carried from the well and heated on the stove, but that was not the real problem. There was simply no place for privacy. We decided not to mention it, lest it become a family affair.

Life in these humble surroundings had to be primitive and uncomplicated. This was the first home in France where we were truly invited guests and we were a little misty-eyed over the experience.

While the good farm wife was preparing the meal, a second daughter came from the village where she had obviously been shopping. She brought material of some sort to make a dress and the two women chattered about the purchase, as they finished preparing the meal. The girl was attractive in a fresh ingenuous way, but reserved with strangers present. Someone sensed that I was a smoker and she brought from the bedroom a packet of the German brand named Faro, holding only three or four. I selected one, as did her father, who immediately thought the occasion called for another drink of the potent schnapps.

Dinner, though plain, was practically a feast to Johnny and me. Living as we did most of the time on cold food, a hot meal of any kind was something special. First came a delicious hot soup, a tasty addition we were to learn that can be found simmering in a pot at the back of the stove in almost every French kitchen. Our appetites, sharpened as they were by the lusty schnapps we had been served, were then amply subdued by sizeable portions of fried potatoes, an egg dish and black bread with butter. Wine seemed to be a measure of hospitality, as it was such an important adjunct to their daily lives. We found it to be true at every level and these people were no exception. The girl had brought their monthly wine ration, which they shared with us. It was altogether a pleasant evening.

After dinner, as Johnny and I mulled over the prospect that these kind people might allow us to sleep in the barn, the mother beckoned us toward the bedroom used by the family. To our surprise, inside the room she stopped short of the door to the barn. She pointed to a four poster single bed in the far corner where Johnny and I could sleep. Toward the middle of the room a few feet away, was a large double bed and, a few feet beyond that in the opposite corner from ours, another four poster single.

My God, I thought, being treated like family was very nice, but extending it to the bedroom was just too much. Surely, the girls would sleep somewhere else. The thought had no more than crossed my mind when the two girls came in and, with no embarrassment, began undressing. Their parents soon joined them. The girls crawled in to the other single bed and the adults into the double.

All this took place while we stood in embarrassed silence. The girls tittered at our obvious quandary and the farmer motioned for us to get to bed. Using a chiffonnier as a shield, we shed our outer garments down to the tattered and filthy underclothes we hadn't been out of for over a month. We were in bed as quickly as possible and our host turned out the light. The family was much amused by our shyness. It was obvious that in families with such sleeping arrangements there would be no false modesty and the facts of life would be learned from infancy — no birds and bees stories for them.

Upon awakening in the morning, we found that the mother had risen early and attempted to darn our sox. They were beyond mending, so she gave us each a pair of her husband's. After we had eaten yet another European style breakfast of half coffee and half cream, served in a bowl with bread, she gave us another precious loaf to take with us. We were well down the road, before we realized that we knew only the first names of these people. Furthermore, we had no mailing address, so we could not express our gratitude in writing, once the conflict was over. We continued on our way, with our hearts as well as our stomachs full.

Johnny and I continued cross country, avoiding roads and population centers whenever possible, for this was working well for us, even in daylight, just so long as the weather stayed dry. As we by-passed St. Mihiel and headed for the city of Commercy, however, what had been a threat all day became a reality and we were drenched with an absolute deluge. If we were to endure walking at all in this downpour, it appeared that we would have to leave the forests and the fields for better conditions. Between us and Switzerland was a large canal, part of the upper Meuse River system, which we must cross. To accomplish this, but not without some trepidation, we began walking one of those heavily travelled paved arteries leading into the industrial city of Commercy.

Fortunately for us, few people were out on Sunday, as we passed through the city in the middle of the day. This being prime occupation zone for the German war machine, however, we began to encounter more and more soldiers in uniform. The center of Commercy seemed like a veritable military base, but, in spite of our tacky appearance, we did not once feel that we were being scrutinized. We walked boldly

No Man's Land

down main streets and through railroad yards without a challenge. Lady Luck walked beside us and we were able to maintain our course without having to detour.

As the urban sprawl faded into the suburbs, we turned South at the city limits toward Vaucouliers, in order to avoid the heavy industrial area of Toul. We had eaten the last bit of bread given to us by the family at Pierrefitte and needed to scrounge for more, as well as for a place to sleep. Pugny, the place where we would cross the Meuse canal, seemed a likely spot.

The weather took a turn for the better and our clothes began to dry out. Nature had given us the bath we needed, although a less than satisfactory one. When we reached the canal crossing, we saw a pair of young lovers strolling along the canal bank. Arms intertwined, their faces carefree, they seemed untouched by what was going on in their country. They smiled as we passed and we responded with "Bon Jour" in our best French manner. There must be something about American enunciation that quickly tags them as foreigners, or maybe these young people, so filled with love for each other, were looking at the world through rose colored glasses. At any rate, they paused and the young woman began talking to us. Of course we couldn't understand half what she said and our reply in halting French interposed with English quickly revealed our identity. The young woman was delighted and began an animated conversation in our language.

Once they understood our plight, they quickly offered help. The young man knew of an abandoned shack not far away and, after they had deposited us there, the two of them went in quest of food for us. In about a half hour the young man returned with bread and cheese, the best he could come up with on such short notice. It became obvious he had left his lady behind for a purpose, for, as Johnny and I ate and warmed ourselves around a small fire, he lingered on. Though he could speak no English, he managed to make us understand that he was about to be conscripted for service in the German army. He wanted to know when the war would end, the coming invasion and what it was like in America. It was obvious that the young French, like the Belgians and the Luxembourgers, were equally distraught over the dim prospects under the Nazis. In this young man's feelings of betrayal, it was easy to recognize the gathering storm of rebellion that would soon envelope the German occupation. There was little we could do to ease the anger and resentment within him, other than assure him the Allies would come in due time. We thanked him for his help and he left.

The next morning, under sunny skies, we set out on the highway to Vaucouliers. We would have to cross another bridge there. We made the crossing at noon and then left the main road to travel across country again to Autreville. We passed through miles and miles of dark woods. These, unlike the others were devoid of underbrush, more like parks. Periodically we came upon encampments with lean-to's, where wood cutters lived. Large piles of slash were waiting to be put in burning pits, where they were reduced to charcoal and then sorted into bins according to size. Nothing was wasted and that accounted for the debris free forest floor.

At day's end we stopped at one of these camps to put out our usual plea for food. Two bearded and grizzled men, their tattered clothes worse than our own, welcomed us without hesitation. They obviously were happy to have visitors and a change of pace. We learned that one was a Pole and the other a Frenchman. The Pole offered me a cigarette almost immediately and, when he discovered my addiction, kept me supplied throughout the evening. While the rest of us warmed ourselves at the fire, the Frenchman put together a stew. He threw in beef trimmings, potatoes, onions, rutabagas and barley, stirred them into a cooked slurry and came up with a gourmet special.

The rest of the evening we spent around the fire, talking and smoking. The Frenchman told us that our planes had bombed Epinal, less than 100 kilometers from here, just a night or two before. He said that huge fires had been started and many people were killed. When he advised us that he had lived in Epinal for a part of his life and had many friends there, a hush in the conversation ensued. Johnny and I felt awkward, even guilty, that we had accepted this man's hospitality, while at the same time our people were killing his friends. The Pole eased the situation when he began relating horror stories about what the Nazis had done to his family near Warsaw. He was the only survivor out of a family of five. Now, four years later, he was here in France by other than his own choosing. The volatile moment passed but talk had become difficult and we made ourselves as comfortable as possible near the fire, and were soon asleep.

After a good breakfast of dark bread and eggs, we bid our hosts goodbye. There was much handshaking as they wished us well and we set off on our hike to Autreville. We were making pretty good time on a country road, when a wood cutter driving a two oxen team, overtook us. We exchanged "Beau jours" and he offered us a ride. He said he was on his way to the next town, Chatanois. Since that fit our plan nicely, we eagerly accepted. Riding on an oxcart turned out to be little better than walking but the time went by fast, for our driver, filled with loneliness from his work, kept up a constant chatter. At first he spoke of everyday events, things that we could understand and answer with a smile oui, oui or non, non. When he realized that we weren't going to contribute anything to the conversation, he began quizzing us about who we were and where we were going.

Since it was only a little after noon, we hadn't yet thought about looking for a place to eat or sleep, but I decided that this friendly fellow might be a good prospect. After I explained that we were American pilots, he became very excited and, with many effusive gestures, confirmed his love for the Allies and his hatred of the Nazis. He became even more attentive and insisted that we stop over at his house in Chatanois.

It turned out that the woodcutter's daughter, all the family he had, ran a small cafe in town about a block from their house. Obviously impressed by his far from impressive looking passengers, he drove down the street of the cafe and called for his daughter in a lusty voice. She came immediately and he spoke quietly to her. After she had learned his little secret, she was as friendly and charitable as her father and indicated she would come to the house later and prepare us a dinner.

When the man had urged the oxen down the street to his house and stabled the beasts in a shed, he pointed to the loft overhead and pantomimed that we could sleep there in the hay. There was little this hard working family could do to entertain us under these wartime conditions, but the warmth they extended in their little home and the simple but tasty meal the daughter prepared gave us the feeling that we were honoring them by our very presence.

We enjoyed a good sleep in the warm hay loft and in the morning ate the usual European breakfast, which we had come to find quite satisfying. Before going on our way, we were presented with a packet of boiled eggs and slices of bread. The warmth and genuine caring of this pair was something we carried away in our hearts, to be long remembered.

Life seemed to be getting better for us, as the weather improved, and we had not been refused food for several days. We had evidently become hardened to the rigors of foot travel, for we were knocking off the miles without any particular discomfort. Our breakfast and lunch kept us going the entire day. It wasn't until we reached Charmois, possibly twenty miles from where we started, that we once more began to think of food.

As we entered the outskirts, we spied a likely looking

house in an isolated section. A plump, ruddy faced young woman responded to my knock. She obviously had been busy in the kitchen, as she was wiping her flour dusted hands on her apron. When we explained our situation, her face lit up and she delightedly welcomed us in. This kind of open reception, which we had received so many times recently, continued to amaze me.

In a mixture of French and broken English, she told us that her husband was the town constable. Then, when she noticed our shocked expressions, she quickly allayed our fears by stating emphatically, "We are French, not German."

At dusk her husband arrived, a robust, good humored man, but wearing, instead of a uniform, the same shabby work clothes that we had seen on most all of the towns people in these parts. With not even a badge to proclaim his office, we wondered how he got by without looking the part. He received us with warmth and good cheer, putting us immediately at ease. Although dinner was of somewhat skimpy portions of boiled potatoes, noodles, scrambled eggs and bread in this poor home, the constable brought out a special vintage Burgundy that he had been saving, for this was the ultimate in French hospitality. Even our unsophisticated tongues appreciated his hospitality.

After dinner he turned the conversation from what had been a jovial light exchange to the more serious topic concerning the bombing of Epinal. His attitude hinted that, since Johnny and I were involved with airplanes, we should have somehow persuaded our peers to direct the destruction against the Germans on German soil, rather than against the French. They too had friends there and had not yet learned of their fate. It seemed to be common knowledge that many people had been killed.

It was plain that these people, like the others, were beginning to feel that the Allies, in their zeal to destroy the German, would wipe the whole of Europe off the map, before they would actually begin what the French considered all important, "The Invasion." The Invasion was of capital importance and was the subject of much speculation. In the face of death and destruction, it was difficult, bordering the impossible, to convince them that the bombings were necessary in order to reduce Allied losses when they began storming the French coastline. The people were suffering and they were chafing to get at the oppressors and destroy them but were helpless. Their only hope would be the invading forces.

The constable's wife, uneasy with the tenor of the conversation, turned the subject back to more mundane matters. After I told her about my wife and the baby that was due in a month, she asked Johnny about his family, or if he had any girl friends. The subject of girls always brought a blush to his face and he feigned disinterest. Shyly he told her he lived with his parents and had no girl friends. It occurred to me then that I actually knew very little about Clarence Wieseckel. He came out of the unknown; we had traveled all these miles together under the most difficult circumstances and I still knew practically nothing about him. He hadn't talked about his childhood, what his interests were, or even about the members of his crew. He was a remarkably private person, but I knew with certainty that, without him, I would have undoubtedly fallen by the wayside. His determination, his integrity, and yes, his devotion kept us going in the face of odds that would have spelled defeat to most anyone else I knew. As little as I knew about him, his efforts had helped us survive the ordeal thus far and that was good enough for me.

That night we were given a blanket apiece and allowed to sleep on the floor in the front portion of the house. In the morning it was again Cafe-creme with bread and jam. When we left, several slices of bread were pressed on us. In our travel, as we became more and more aware of what these people were enduring, we realized how precious the food was they shared with us. Even in the face of our need, we felt a little guilty in accepting it.

After examining the map, we figured we would be approximately a mile South of Epinal at noon. We intended to circumvent the bombed out city and hoped to reach Plombiers at day's end. About eleven o'clock, experiencing our usual apprehension, when approaching populated areas, even more so here where we anticipated seeing the destruction left behind by our bombers, we were making our way over a broad wooded hill that commanded a good view of the entire industrial area. Up to this point, we had not seen any sign of bomb damage. Down in the valley below us, the only sign of activity, a steam locomotive was pulling a dozen freight cars, chugging along a track that led to Epinal less than a mile away.

Suddenly, from out of nowhere, came one of our own Mustang fighter planes, streaking along behind the train at tree top level. From our vantage point we had a panoramic view of the drama. There was a tremendous roar and rattle of his fifty calibre machine guns as he strafed the train from back to front. Although there was no explosion, the train came to an abrupt halt. The locomotive sat there like a wounded dragon, with steam mushrooming above the tracks and billowing up to our level. Evidently the pilot could make no more than one pass, for he didn't return. We watched as the steam diminished to a few wisps. We could only assume that some of the crew hadn't survived, or the locomotive was put out of commission. This was the total summary of destruction from the air that we were able to witness around Epinal.

It was an exciting experience for us to see one of our own fighter planes in action at ground level. This was not just practice; it was for real. We were thrilled with the audacity of the move and knew that it was largely up to the pilot what target he chose. Some planes were equipped with cameras, not only to record the accuracy of such moves, but to provide material for later critiques.

The rest of the day went by without further incident and we continued to make good time on our hike toward Plombiers. We stopped to rest in a field and a young farm lad of about twelve happened along. In typical unabashed boy fashion, he stopped to ask us what we were doing here on his father's farm. There wasn't much point in giving this empty handed young boy our usual spiel, but Johnny answered his question by opening up our map, pointing to Plombiers as our destination and then to us.

"Vous Americans?" the boy fairly exploded with excitement. He must have heard family talk about Americans coming soon. He said something that sounded like, "Je domo Plombiers." We took it to mean that he lived in the town and this farm was part of the settlement. He pointed to a house up on a hill behind us and motioned us to come with him. For the boy, we were a prize to be shown to his parents; for us, it was surely an invitation to a meal. When we reached the house, the boy shouted "Americans!" and stood beside us with pride, when his mother opened the door.

The mother studied us from the doorway, being considerably more cautious than her young son. Her expression changed as she took in our bedraggled condition, and compassion overrode caution. She welcomed us with warmth and immediately her concern was for our comfort. She motioned us to chairs, as she left to get her husband who was in the barn. He came and greeted us, seemingly with no regard for our appearance, and soon proffered us an invitation to dinner. It seemed that being American fliers was the open sesame to the people's hospitality. I wondered how much of it we could lay to the fact that we were Americans and how much was their desire to thwart the Nazis, who would surely take into custody downed Americans, if they were aware of our presence.

We joined the family at the kitchen basin to wash before dinner and discovered that there was a younger son and a teenage daughter. In almost no time we were accepted into this gentle family with no question. They made us feel that we belonged there. After we had gathered around the table and said grace, the dishes of food were passed around as casually as if we had been there many times. This well organized family was not given to small talk. Eating was serious business and there was little conversation as we ate. It was enough that we were accepted as part of the machinations of war and they were giving us sustenance to further the war effort. We were part of what would eventually come—the Invasion.

When we had eaten our fill, the farmer led us to the hayloft and bid us goodnight. Before we slept, Johnny and I reflected on the kindness of all the rural people who had helped us on our way. In the oft repeated 23rd Psalm, the passage reads, "Thou preparest a table before me in the presence of mine enemies; thou anointed my head with oil; my cup runneth over."

We agreed, we certainly had been fed right under the noses of the enemy and, while we hadn't been anointed with oil, our cup certainly was filled and running over—with gratitude. With a certain humbleness, I drifted off to sleep.

The Girl From Melissey

As we started out again from Plombiers, the month of May was nearly at an end. In the twelve days since we left the Partisan camp we had literally been put through an endurance test. Bit by bit we were gaining strength from the good food given to us in our role as beggars and we had gradually built up endurance that we didn't have when we started out. Without realizing it, we were experiencing a subtle change. The bad part was behind us now and, with the warm sun shining almost daily, it was great just to be alive. The fresh green hills and lush valleys, with their meandering streams filled with their early Spring runoff, were not marred by the pox of war. Moreover, the forests and hills seemed to conspire with the country folk to offer us protection, almost as if they were waiting for our passage. Navigation became a snap, when we learned that a steel towered transmission line we picked up in Plombiers would be with us all the way to Switzerland. We had traversed the Western terrain as shown on Johnny's map and would now turn it over to seek directions on the Eastern side.

As we came to a small but steep range of mountains on course, we began climbing it with unabated energy, happy to find that we experienced no difficulty. About mid-day, it was our surprise and good fortune to find a farmhouse deep within the mountains, and we wasted no time seeking an invitation to lunch. We were well received by the French housewife and she served us German pancakes, further testimonial of cross cultural lore continually cropping up in our travels. When we had finished eating, we hiked down the other side of the mountain to a protected valley at the bottom.

In search of a certain road on Johnny's map, we crossed a meadow sprinkled with wild flowers. There, not far from the town of Melissey, we came to a large, handsome farmhouse concealed from view from its neighbors. Villa might better describe it, for it had a red tile roof over dazzling white walls, in which were set English style mullioned windows. The whole place had an air of prosperity. We were in need of additional information at this point and were happy to see a slender young lady step gracefully through the front gate. Our timing was perfect and this very attractive girl answered our questions graciously and in English, not the least bit stand offish in face of our disreputable appearance. Her blue eyes held a mischievous glint and her peaches and cream complexion and sensuous red lips added to her typically chic French look. Her honey blonde hair was cropped off in a boyish bob and she dressed in plain country girl style with little or no makeup. To cap it off, she had a fabulous figure befitting such a lovely creature.

My poor attempt at French had labeled me immediately as a foreigner. "You are Americans, aren't you?" she said, making it a statement rather than a question. Her voice was clear and melodious, with no hint of artifice.

I had been somewhat bemused since we first spied her and was only too happy to converse with her. "Yes, my name is Don and this is Johnny. We are fliers and were shot down several weeks ago. We have walked all the way from Belgium."

She seemed delighted to have someone her own age to speak English with, considering that French was undoubtedly her native tongue. She spoke English very well. She looked steadily at me and took no notice of my shabby clothes—and no notice at all of Johnny. He might as well not have been there as far as she was concerned, even though he was a far more eligible candidate for her attentions than I. But, of course, she didn't know that.

"Where will you go? You cannot get back to England from here."

"We're heading for Switzerland," I explained and wondered why she thought we had any choice.

"But the war will be over soon. They will not let you leave Switzerland. It will be too late to let you be of any service," she announced, as if she had struck upon an idea.

"Well, we have to try. No one knows where we are or even if we are alive."

"That's the point," she interrupted. "No one is expecting you to return, so you will not have to. You can stay right here in this house. We have plenty of room and there is food enough. When the invasion comes, then you can return."

"That would be very nice, but there are people who want to know that we are safe. When one is listed as 'missing in action', no one knows whether he is alive or dead. If we reach Switzerland, we can get word to them."

Through all this exchange, she kept her attention on me. Her every move, her tone of voice and, most of all, her eyes made me realize the little minx was attempting to seduce me. Any man alive would have been flattered by her attentions and I was no exception. I loved the whole by-play but Johnny's soft voice broke the hypnotic spell. "I think we had better get going. It's getting late."

The invitation was a tremendous temptation. After all, hadn't we in effect completed our hitch when we were shot down? What more could be expected of us? Why should we put ourselves back into another hell hole, when we had already managed to survive one? I had to admit to myself that the whole scenario: 'boy meets girl and just like that, "bingo," he chucks everything', was outlandish. I didn't know whether Johnny was aware of the electricity that was crackling between us or not.

I couldn't honestly say it was one sided and, for a moment, what she proposed had seemed possible. War brings out an urgency in all relations, a desire to make the most of everything while you can, for there may be no tomorrow. But there was something far more important than a dalliance with this lovely temptress: My destiny with Johnny had yet to be fulfilled. Destiny had thrown us together and nothing short of capture by the Nazis could keep us from making our escape to Switzerland. We thanked the beautiful lady and, not without some reluctance for me, said goodbye, as we went on our way again.

Since the pace we were setting along the valley road to Melissey was fairly brisk in the afternoon heat, we decided to ask for water at the first prospect close to the town. In the first block at the outskirts, we saw a short chubby man hoeing a garden patch between two houses. To our surprise, he waved to us in a friendly way and pointed down the street in the direction we were travelling. We couldn't understand why he should be giving us such attention and continued on. In the next block, at the gate of a tidy home, another even more friendly gentleman greeted us. He smiled and beckoned us to come in. We were completely nonplussed. What possible explanation could there be for this unsolicited welcome?

"Vi 'ave vaited for you," he announced, as he ushered us in the front door. Inside, his wife, a large matronly woman, greeted us warmly. Their accent was heavier than French, more like German, but they spoke to each other in French. (We learned later that the heavier accent made it easier for us to understand.) While the greeting and welcome had been fast, I still had time to question this strange reception. Hadn't he said they were expecting us?

"Oui, oui, vous Americans? Yes?" he asked in broken French and English.

"How did you know?" was my response. I was looking for an answer to this riddle.

"Ah ha!" he laughed and tapped his temple as though he had some special divining power.

"Vous American," he stated positively, pointing at me. "Vous Francaise," pointing at Johnny.

From a nearby magazine rack, his wife plucked a well-thumbed publication. Quickly she opened it to a men's clothing ad, featuring several male models. "Vous blonde, Hollywood," she said, pointing to me. "Vous Francaise," she said, holding up the page toward Johnny and pointing to a brunette model.

It was obvious she, like many Europeans, had over simplified the identification of Americans, probably from seeing too many American movies. We laughed and the incident passed, but we were still in a quandary. We searched for an answer. How about the man with the hoe up the street? In the last day or two curtains had moved at windows, indicating people were watching our passage. We were approaching the Swiss border and perhaps they were accustomed to seeing victims of the war straggling through their towns. But there was another possibility. Had the girl from Melissey somehow got word to these people? Maybe she herself had received advance warning of our coming and made plans with the neighbors to ask us to stay at her house. Had she set up this welcoming committee? I shrugged off the idea, but wanted an answer to still another question and turned to our host. "If you knew us to be Americans, me in particular, why hadn't the Germans also been perceptive?"

"Non, non, non, non," he laughed with almost childlike glee. "Le Boche stupid. He not see, but Francaise—" and tapped his temple again to indicate superior intelligence.

This house was like a middle income American home, loaded with overstuffed furniture, fancy gate leg tables and walls adorned with paintings and tapestries. They insisted we spend the night. Upon readily accepting the invitation, we were shown to a bedroom which held fine furniture and was equipped with hand painted China bowls for wash basins and, painted to match, a large China chamber pot with a lid. It seemed strange that, even in this more affluent home, there was no inside plumbing. The chamber pot, the most elaborately adorned I had ever seen, was for my own personal use and turned out to be a life saver. During the night, my dysentery problem made itself known, probably initiated by the deliciously rich dinner served by our hostess.

During the course of the meal, we were told that arrangements were being made for a car to take us to the border. We didn't know of any organized patriots at this point but certainly wouldn't turn down a ride, if one were forthcoming. In the morning, our elderly host advised that the deal had fallen through, but he would personally escort us on foot to the village of Fras, about four kilometers distant. There he would turn us over to a member of the "Resistance," a name we concluded was part of the "Underground." The man owned a wine distributorship in nearby Champagny.

When we arrived in Fras, we learned that our contact had to be away on business, but he had instructed his mother and daughter to give us aid. They both spoke English very well and, with this improved communication, we soon learned that our impression of their being an organized Underground was entirely erroneous. We had already said goodbye to our kind host from Melissey and now learned from the mother and daughter that he had a flair for the dramatic and had overplayed the entire idea. There was no such organization, but the two women treated us well and gave us excellent directions to the Swiss border. With their blessing, we took our leave and were on our own once more.

That evening we had no trouble at all finding a farmhouse near Champagny, where we were given a good meal and the use of a hayloft to make our bed. It served to confirm our belief that these people were used to seeing survivors of military crashes and help was extended whenever contacts were made. The next morning the farmer Samaritan directed us to Hericourt, less than a day's walk ahead.

When we arrived at the village, we were actually greeted openly by members of a French Underground that must have been working more or less independently. One of them was a comely middle-aged woman who spoke perfect English. We learned that she was here to be with her husband who was deeply involved with the resistance movement. Their four children were with their grandmother in St. Mihiel. Displaced families seemed to be the norm rather than the unusual, as so many were uprooted by conditions under the oppressors.

Quickly the woman explained the situation, "I will take you to an abandoned house here in Hericourt where you will stay until guides are available to take you across the border. Others are waiting there, some Indians of the British army who fled from Epinal when your bombers came and some Yugoslavians who deserted from the German-Russian front."

She was very open and business-like. There was no effort made to conceal our presence or hide our destination. When she escorted us, instead of an effort toward concealment or cloak and dagger tactics, she walked us boldly along the sidewalks of Hericourt, as if she owned the place. She said she would be back later to take us to a carnival now in full swing at nearby Mandeure. A carnival! The very idea seemed incongruous.

When we arrived at the house, we were met with a great round of hand shaking and back slapping, as the motley crew gathered to greet us. Anyone watching would have thought we had just won a marathon race. There were many joyful exclamations and, with everyone talking at once, the din they created could have been heard for blocks. Nearly everyone spoke English, at least to some degree. If the Germans had a detachment of military police in the area, the group was practically asking to be captured. There was plenty of beer and tobacco to enliven the party and undoubtedly the beer was partly responsible for the elevated noise level.

The lady from St. Mihiel brought a prune pie for our lunch. It didn't take us long to dispose of it. Our new friends made every effort to make us comfortable but the afternoon seemed to drag, as we impatiently waited for instructions from the underground. For Johnny and me, the battle would not be won until we were safely across the border. Some of these men, particularly the Indians, had been involved in the conflict since the invasion of Poland. Their campaign had begun in Greece and they had not been home in five years. They seemed to view us as heroes, because America represented their hope for liberation.

At the end of the day, Johnny and I were taken to a farmhouse where an excellent meal awaited us and a good bed to sleep in. The generous and most accommodating lady of the house brought us tubs of hot water in which to bathe our feet and, while we slept, washed our clothes. There seemed to be no end to the generosity and manifest thoughtfulness of these people.

The next day we continued to congratulate ourselves, knowing that in all probability we would be crossing the border on the morrow, May 30th. The lady who had greeted us so openly arrived to fulfill her promise to take us to the carnival. This time, her husband, a slender kinky-haired Frenchman, was with her. She introduced him to us as Renee. They had balanced extra bicycles alongside the ones they rode. Once we had mounted them, they told us they wanted to take us on a little side trip. I found it true that the art of riding a bicycle, once learned, is never forgotten. We were soon pedaling along with our guides and enjoying the experience.

Our destination turned out to be a cemetery on the outskirts of Hericourt. There, among stone monuments marking the graves of many generations of citizens, were six freshly painted white crosses, marking the final resting places of crewmen from an English Lancaster bomber. Our escorts explained that an English R.A.F. pilot, four Canadians, and a Frenchman rested there. Their plane had crashed not far from Hericourt. It was a sobering moment for Johnny and me and made us realize even more deeply how fortunate we were. Perhaps only split seconds separated us, standing here alive and well, from those six young men lying at our feet. If fortune had been with them, they could be with us when we made our way across the border. We were all the more anxious to hasten what to us could be the biggest challenge of all, crossing the border to the haven of Swiss neutrality, and then home.

After a few moments of poignant silence, we mounted our bicycles and went on to Mandeure, where we were to meet one of the top leaders of the Resistance, before going to the carnival. It took us only a short time to pedal the four kilometers. The meeting place was a house near the town square, where the carnival was in progress. The sound of a calliope invaded our less than festive mood. For me, at least, the tootling tunes of a calliope heralded a time of light heartedness and always summoned forth memories of happy childhood. Now it seemed irritatingly brash and insensitive. "The Woodpecker Serenade" piped out into the Spring air was counterfeit, a veneer over the serious business at hand.

The commander, a lean young Frenchman sporting a crew cut, greeted us. When he extended his right hand, I then realized that his left sleeve hung empty. Almost violet blue eyes that would have been the envy of many a girl, seemed incongruous above a Mussolini like jaw and a mouth with a slightly cruel twist. In spite of his warm greeting, I found myself thinking I would not want to have this man for an enemy; however, he treated us with nothing but compassion. Once we got down to business, he spoke in brief choppy sentences and told us that Renee and another Frenchman would be guiding us to the border. We would ride bicycles to the critical area and then cross on foot. The time was set for the day after tomorrow. Disappointment flooded over me, but I realized that the man's business involved much more than just getting escapees across the border to Switzerland.

With little ceremony, he motioned us to another room where we were served a lunch that seemed quite sumptuous in these troubled times. Wine, beer and cigarettes were lavishly available, making it quite an occasion.

After we had eaten, we sauntered the short distance to the square where gaudy booths were set up. The calliope sounded even louder and people milled around, enjoying the festive occasion. Children, shrieking with excitement, darted through the crowd. Wary eyed, Johnny and I looked for German uniforms, but we didn't see any. It wouldn't have surprised us much if we had, considering the audacious boldness of our hosts. Gradually our mood began to match the light hearted notes of the calliope and we were cheered by the sight of a merry-go-round where happy children lined up, coins in hand, waiting for a turn on the faded and worn steeds. Even so, the whole affair seemed like a pretense to us. How could life be so frivolous, when we had actually witnessed the hardships going on all around us. Also this seemed like a celebration ahead of winning a race, for we were not yet safe across the border.

Our friends were marvelous hosts and after a while sensed our mood and took us to the home of another of their members. He was a wiry old fellow who immediately made us feel welcome. He prepared for us a first class dinner around lean beef and we had all the port wine we could drink. We stayed the night and the next night as well. We slept well, in a real bed with mattress and springs. In the morning, he served us a Cafe-creme breakfast and then busied himself in his little garden, leaving us to our own devices.

Time for us inched by interminably. We felt like runners, anxious to get into our starting blocks and it was an effort not to pace the floor. We did a sort of mental calisthenics, getting ourselves in shape for this last crucial lap of our long journey. We had time to recap our good fortune, ticking off incidents, generosities and kindnesses one by one. Our worn out shoes had been replaced by someone who may have needed them more than we did. We had been given food and drink in times of great need. The people along our way had even administered to our wounded travel-worn feet. We felt great affection for these generous people of France. One more thought came to mind: Yesterday we rode bicycles we hadn't had to steal.

Victory and Tragedy

The old man awakened us early on the 31st of May, so we could have breakfast before our guides arrived. Renee soon appeared at the door with an associate whom he introduced as Michel. They each had an extra bicycle for our use. After bidding adieu to the kind old gentleman, we headed toward Montbelliard, a way point on the trek to the border. We weren't as muscle toned to cycling as our guides, but soon found we had little difficulty keeping pace.

After almost a week of sunshine, the skies were overcast, a welcome circumstance, as we strained up the gradually increasing slopes leading to the mountains. The guides finally stopped at a remote spot. The rest of the way, they said, was too steep for bicycle travel. We stashed them in some brush and proceeded on foot. Michel took the lead, as he had made the trip many times. Renee followed fifty paces behind, close enough to relay signals to us. We brought up the rear with fifty paces between us. In case of a surprise, this strategy provided the maximum protection.

Renee was a light hearted fellow but his disdain of the Germans was graphically illustrated when he sneered the word "Le Bosche" and spat through his teeth, leaving no doubt about his feelings toward them. Both he and Michel carried revolvers inside their shirts, indicating that this was no light hearted venture.

We held to the mountain trail for a while and suddenly Renee signalled for us to maintain silence, as we were nearing the critical border area. We had been walking for nearly two hours and it was approaching noon. Michel led us off the main trail and we walked through open virgin forest. The forest floor, covered with a mat of twigs and dead leaves was very dry underfoot. It was impossible to walk quietly. The snap of every twig, the crackle of every leaf was magnified in the clear mountain air. Alert to the danger of the situation, we wanted to pause after each step. As we neared the end of our climb, Michel disappeared into a dense grove of trees, but passed a signal to Renee, who motioned with his hands that we were near the border. Then Renee too disappeared from our view.

Suddenly, two rifle shots rang out from a short distance ahead and to the right of where Michel had disappeared. There were no cries of halt or shouts of warning. Momentarily stunned, we stood in disbelief for a few precious seconds.

We hadn't come this far to finally stand and wait for capture. Our well-oiled reflexes galvanized us into headlong flight down the mountain in the direction from which we had just come. In great panting leaps we searched for cover. First Johnny would be in the lead and then I would overtake and pass him and then he would pass me. We must have gone a mile in such fashion, before we finally found brush heavy enough to conceal us. We dived in like a couple of rabbits into a briar patch. We huddled together, breathing in chest heaving gasps and our hearts beat frantically. We had heard no sound from either Michel or Renee. There was no way of knowing whether they had been taken prisoner or were lying dead there on the mountain top.

Gradually our belabored hearts quieted and our breathing returned to normal. We were on our own. An hour passed and there was no sign of Michel or Renee. The German guards had the advantage. They could sit like hunters in a blind and wait for their quarry to approach. The dry forest floor provided them with the perfect alarm system. What were we to do?

There seemed no answer until nature itself came to our rescue.

We could see little of the sky from our position, but suddenly the Spring clouds thickened and a spattering of rain began to fall. All at once it was nearly dark, lightning split open the sky, there was a rumble of thunder and, with a roar, a torrent of rain descended upon us. Within minutes there were rivulets of water on the forest floor. Our soaked condition counted for little, for we were certain that the storm was to our benefit. It would certainly take the snap, crackle and pop out of walking conditions. While the storm raged around us, we formulated a plan to make a wide pass around the dense grove where our guides had disappeared. In that way we should certainly escape detection by the Germans who had shot at them.

Dripping wet, we started the climb back up the mountain, leaving plenty of space to the left of the area where we had last seen our guides. We had no idea how the border would be marked, so we made a cautious approach. This time we walked on the forest floor without making a sound. The element of surprise was no longer in the guards' favor.

We had gone some distance through the dense forest, when we suddenly broke out into a cleared area, a grassy strip some five hundred feet wide, winding its way between heavy forests along the ridge top. There wasn't a scrap of wood left by foresters anywhere along the strip. This just had to be the Swiss border.

We had approached it on a fairly straight line commanding a view in both directions for long distances. It occurred to us that well placed guards, as well as ourselves, could see a considerable distance in all directions. It was too late to turn back, if success was to be ours. We dare not let indecision hinder us now. We agreed to make a run for it. Without looking to the right or to the left, we began our 500 foot dash. We fairly flew across the green meadow, steep as it was. If we had been trying out for the Olympics, both of us would have easily made the team.

With every pounding step we took, we expected shots to be fired, bullets to tear into our flesh. But there were none. Adrenalin gave speed to our feet and determination kept us going into the woods on the opposite side. We reached a forest road that paralleled the border and we chose that as our place to collapse on the ground, completely exhausted.

With senses recovered, I saw from my prone position, first the boots, then as my eyes lifted, the khaki clad figure of a soldier standing a few feet away with rifle slung over his shoulder. My heart lurched and then steadied, when I saw the white cross emblem of Switzerland on his shoulder patch. He was a Swiss soldier and we need fear no longer. We were so jubilant, so relieved, that if he had asked us to kiss the ground we lay upon, we would have happily obeyed. As matters stood, not a word passed between us; he simply pointed down the road in the direction we were to travel. Johnny and I had spent nineteen days and walked six hundred miles to reach this spot.

From here on, our status shifted to a different plane. We were no longer "Missing in action." We could soon cable our families and be reinstated in the blessed category of the living.

The Swiss soldier, who had acted as though he expected us, motioned us to walk beside him. He didn't actually take us into custody but it was plain he wanted to keep an eye on us. From the tiny border town of Damvant, we were whisked away in a lorry to Bade Lostorf, near the German sector town of Porrentruy a few miles away. Bade Lostorf was a chalet type structure used as a quarantine center for all of the European escapees. There were no Germans, but there were the much discredited Italians.

At the beginning of our boring three weeks of detention, we were put through chemical sprays for delousing, like animals run through sheep dip, and then subjected to endless questioning by the suspicious and hard-boiled Swiss. Finally we were given almost prison-like food and shown our straw matted sleeping quarters. The Americans were housed in one wing but mingled with forty or fifty other refugees of all nationalities at meal time. Traffic over the border was heavy and accommodations were strained to the limit. The food was disgusting. Johnny and I had done better when we were living on handouts from the generous French. The treatment we received did nothing toward making us feel welcome. We were ruthlessly regimented and felt virtually prisoners.

While at Bade Lostorf, each of us received a Red Cross packet containing toilet articles and such sundries as needle and thread and paper and pencil. The American Legation was apparently not allowed to pay us a personal visit but, through the Red Cross, it passed on whatever information it had of our crew members. In that way, I learned for certain that it was Leo Carey who was killed. Jack was taken prisoner. The information we had received about Suber, Standridge, Beckham, Butler, and the substitute radio operator, all taken prisoners, was verified. In addition, I learned that Bob and Joe had been captured shortly after they left Johnny and me at Beaumont.

Our military attache, Council General Woods, sent word that we were allowed to cable home, up to ten words, and we were allowed to receive the same. I carefully put together the words I wanted to send Jeanne. They read: "Am safe cable baby's sex name color hair eyes love, Don." I don't know why it was important to know hair and eye color, unless I thought they would indicate whether or not the child looked like me.

Her ten word reply was a masterpiece: "Wonderful news son Greg blonde blue eyes everyone fine love Jeanne." So, I was the father of a son. I was both relieved and happy.

There was absolutely no planned activity at Bade Lostorf, neither were there any newspapers, not even a radio. The hours seemed like days. Johnny and I had made new friends, a beginning of the separation that protocol dictated in matters pertaining to rank. The only real high point of our days was the appearance of a fruit vendor who sold us dried figs and nuts from his push cart.

There were a few Italian officers who had sought asylum, after the defeat of their own axis forces. Why the Swiss put them in with us, we couldn't understand. The first night or two, after we Americans were already seated in the common mess hall, one of the Italian officers sauntered in, wearing riding breeches and shiny boots. His tunic was draped casually over his shoulders and one hand was thrust inside his shirt front, Napoleon style. Our Allied soldiers, a sorry lot for the most part, wore piecemeal uniforms or none at all, but had their arms correctly in their sleeves. The next evening we were ready for him. We tarried long enough to make sure he was there ahead of us. All the Americans and British who could muster up jackets and coats, wore them draped over their shoulders and, with right hands tucked in shirt fronts, solemnly marched into the mess hall. Not a word was said but, from that night on, that officer came in with his arms in his tunic sleeves and there was no Napoleonic affectation. His expensive uniform had set him apart from us in the first place.

At the end of three weeks, we were put aboard a train to our new home in Glion. There was a stopover in Bern, where we were processed at the American Legation. When the paper work was completed, we were each reinstated on the payrolls of our various home bases in England. We were paid the bonus flight pay, just as though we were still in flight. It would continue until we returned, a strange way to handle the situation, but it pleased us. We were then sent to a men's shop to buy civilian clothes. The act of buying clothes of my choice and discarding the odd garments I had worn for so long, did much to restore me.

Before leaving Bern, the Americans were taken before a Swiss military tribunal for their own version of debriefing, but it was obvious they wished to pry from us information that might be useful for their own purposes. We had already been briefed by our military attache as to what sort of questions we could answer and what we could not. However, we were not prepared for the ostentatious military protocol observed by the Swiss military. The officer in charge was obviously regular army for, when we failed to stand when he entered the room, his face turned crimson with anger and he stormed out of the room with all the ramrod stiffness of a Prussian general. Almost immediately, a briefing officer appeared. He too was furious and proceeded to dress us down for our lack of courtesy. When we had been sufficiently reprimanded by this underling, the senior officer made his appearance again and this time we stood up to show our respect but I thought with a tongue in cheek attitude.

We learned later that all able bodied male Swiss were subject to a national conscription law and were required to undergo training each year similar to our National Guard. Military courtesy had a high priority and it was taken for granted that we would have been indoctrinated to the same degree, a faulty premise as far as our raunchy bomber crews were concerned.

This same Prussian discipline carried over to the civilian sector in war time, at least as far as their treatment of Americans was concerned. As Escapees, we were given a curfew of 10:00 P.M. while under military supervision. That evening in Bern, some of our bunch decided to visit a small night club just around the corner from our hotel. It seemed inoffensive enough to us, especially since we had just endured a long confinement away from lights and gaiety. When the 10 o'clock hour arrived, Lt. Tucker and I felt we might be excused if we stayed on a little longer. No more than a half hour elapsed before a Swiss M.P. appeared and quietly ushered us back to the hotel. We congratulated ourselves that no harm had come to us for slightly bending the rules.

About two weeks after we were settled in Glion however, Lt. Tucker and I were confronted in the lobby of de Glion Hotel, which was now our home. Two M.P's carrying rifles read the charges against us and then, giving us only time enough to pack our kits, hauled us off to prison. Conditions were archaic, to put it mildly, and we lived on bread and soup for the next ten days. The tedium was lightened about the third or fourth day, when an influential businessman was thrown in with us for an equally minor infraction. At least we were consoled by the thought that we weren't having to rub elbows with common criminals. This fellow had been late reporting for his annual military training. He spoke English and we immediately became friends. Many lively exchanges ensued and the last days of our internment were bearable. Our sentence completed, he invited us to spend a night at his palatial lake front home in Lausanne.

Back at Glion, the American contingent now numbered two hundred or more and were divided into two groups, the newer arrivals assigned to de Glion Hotel. Since we all wore civilian clothes, there was no distinguishable difference between officers and enlisted men. The difference showed up in the room assignments and seating arrangements in the dining room. The natural effect was that little cliques were inevitably established and the military caste system was maintained, even though we had no military duties to perform. It seemed to me that the enlisted men were happy with the arrangement, for some officers were obnoxious enough that, on occasion, I'd have as soon been an enlisted man myself.

This continued observance of protocol made it awkward to maintain the relationship that had developed between Johnny and me. Under our new existence, his personality further served to isolate us. Being as shy and retiring as he was, he wouldn't push to continue a relationship he felt had ended once the officer, enlisted man barrier was again in place. In addition, I must confess to a certain "laissez faire," for I had automatically drifted into associations with men with whom I had more common interests.

Johnny and I had shared a unique experience. I don't know that either of us expected we would continue the very special intimacy that developed during our sometimes harrowing trek from Belgium to Switzerland. What had happened, how we felt about it, could never be understood by anyone else. Back in our circumscribed world, we weren't the same people. I knew even then that I was a different man than I was when I dropped from the sky and landed on the soil of Luxembourg. Johnny and our shared experiences would forever be a part of me, probably the greatest experience I'd ever have.

The grapevine gossip was true, the invasion finally took place. Patton led his Seventh Army through Southern France to Lyon. During the mop up stage, he sent trucks to the Swiss border, where we "Escapees" were picked up and eventually returned to our bases. There we were given a choice of being reassigned to another combat zone, or returned to the States to serve as flying instructors.

Lt. Tucker and I chose to come back to the States and were routed to Washington, D.C. for interrogation. It seemed that the State Department wanted to know more about the circumstances of our arrest and imprisonment. The upshot of it was, the curfew incident was recognized as a very minor infraction and an apology was extracted from the Swiss government for the drastic treatment we received.

When all of the formalities were taken care of, I was given leave to visit Jeanne and my five-months-old son. Thus ended that stress-filled, sometimes violent, sometimes strange, sometimes wonderful period of my life.

Leo Carey
gravestone

Died in Toye's bomber crash
Luxembourg graveyard

Epilogue

All of the surviving crew members of "Nine Yanks and a Jerk," who were on that fateful mission to Munich, were released from prison and returned home after the war. Leo Carey, the man we felt carried the mark of death, was buried at Hamm cemetery in Belgium. Later on, a service was held for him at the Catholic Church in Lieler, Luxembourg with me and my family in attendance.

That night in 1944 at the Fairon's house, when Jean Freres held up two fingers that indicated two people had died in the crash, I had thought one of them was Jack Farmer. I learned that, instead of Jack, the second casualty was a little girl playing with a friend in an amphitheater-shaped field. Our ship, missing the wing that had been blown off, came in on a circular pattern, belching flames and scattering debris, as it bounced a couple of times and exploded. The child was so terrified that she literally died of fright.

Except for a single visit from Bob Korth, our navigator, I have contacted the other members of my crew only through letters. It seemed we shared a mutual feeling that our war experiences were something we'd just as soon forget.

Among the many letters I received from those wonderful Partisans in Luxembourg, Belgium and France after the war, there was one from Renee's wife, the Renee who was one of the guides who led us to the Swiss border. Renee was killed the day of our border crossing. But because of the language barrier, it wasn't clear to me in her letter whether he was killed by one of the shots we heard that day or died from the effects of a brutal beating given him by the Germans as they attempted to extract information concerning his organization. We learned that Michel, who had led us up the mountain, was Renee's uncle. He was taken prisoner and set to hard labor. He escaped and evened the score near the war's end by killing many Germans. The opportunity came during the routing of occupation forces in his home town. The Nazis soon learned it was better to be taken prisoner by the Americans than to fall into the hands of the vengeful Partisans.

In their first letter to us after the war, the Fairons let us know what happened to the Luxembourg boys who were hiding in the cave where Bob Korth and Joe Kerpan were taken immediately following the crash. The day after Bob and Joe were removed for the rendezvous with me at the Fairon house, the Germans discovered the cave and ruthlessly killed the five boys. The Luxembourgers suffered terribly under the yoke of the Germans and in addition bore the brunt of the heavy bombardments from General Rundstedt's offensive, during the battle of the bulge.

I must add that some years after the end of the war, Clarence Wieseckel and his wife visited me at my home in Portland, Oregon. They hoped my wife Jeanne and I would join them on a trip to Europe to follow the trek "Johnny" and I had made from Belgium to Switzerland, and in the process, contact the people who had befriended us. At the time, we weren't financially able to join them.

The visit was a disturbing one for me. I could find in Clarence no vestige of the Johnny with whom I had walked in the rain, hidden in ditches, forests and barns with, broke bread with, and clung to in the darkness of foreign countries. He was Clarence Wieseckel, middle class American, with nothing to set him apart from many others.

Clarence died in 1981. He had raised a family, done well in the company with which he was associated and now was dead, too soon, it seemed to me. But then there was "Johnny" to deal with. Had he died too? Was he the Clarence who paid us the visit? Why did I continue to think of these two as different from each other? Was it possible they were not one and the same?

My life had moved along unexpected paths. My three children were grown and on their own, and my marriage had ended. A second marriage brought much happiness and, along with it, a desire to do what Clarence had wanted, a trip to Europe. So, my wife and I, along with her son, daughter-in-law, who speaks French and German, and their young daughter made the trip together. A belated memorial service for Leo Carey was held at the church in Lieler, Luxembourg, with us in attendance, an event that had been put aside for thirty-seven years.

One by one, we visited the Fairons, the Freres and the Kirches. The time we spent with them, their friendliness, their joy at my return, combined to make a succession of moving experiences. When we finally wound up in Glion, it was a shock to find that some of the fine resort hotels had been torn down and the whole community had a generally seedy and run down appearance. I discovered that, if I stood at the edge of the parking lot that now marked where Hotel de Glion had once stood, I could get the same view of Lake Geneva I had enjoyed from my seat in the dining room. With mixed emotions I gazed at the scene and dwelt on my memories.

This trip to Europe had brought home to me the old maxim that you can't turn back the hands of time. I hadn't found "Johnny" in Clarence Wieseckel and I hadn't found him along the route we had traveled together. Reason told me that Clarence had dropped out of the skies, dangling from a parachute, just as I had. But there were many times I felt it had been wings that brought him. Now, looking over the blue waters of the lake, I knew that "Johnny" was given birth by the times. The person I knew as "Johnny" was a side of Clarence, probably even he didn't know was there. He did what he felt he had to do. He saved me from capture or worse. Shy, retiring Clarence became "Johnny," who in the face of terrible odds, forged on, pulling me with him. In the process he saved Clarence Wieseckel. I know with certainty that "Johnny" didn't die with Clarence Wieseckel. He would always live in a special place in my heart.

What was less certain was what had prompted those people who represented the enemy along the way, to act as they had. There were guards, gendarmes and the men in the black sedan who had seen us, who surely had been aware that we weren't supposed to be where we were. In fact, I had seen a flicker of that awareness in their eyes. I seem to remember reading somewhere that sometimes animals, when confronted by another animal, will look the other way, as if to say, "If I pretend I don't see you, I won't have to do anything about it." The enemy had literally looked the other way.

What prompted them to act as they had? Was it the Divine Providence I felt had intervened when our ship was shot down? What about the people who had fed and clothed us and given us shelter? Perhaps there was a little of the Divine, made manifest in each and every one of them.

When we returned from Europe, a certain restlessness came over me. It was as if "Johnny" were prompting me to finish what I had started thirty-seven years before. I resurrected the manuscript that had been gathering dust, so to speak, all that time. I could almost hear him saying, as he had so many times when we were in France together, "Come on, Don. You can do it."

"So here it is, Johnny. I have finished it."